B²

The Old Art and New Science of
the Business Network

A. J. Marr

Introduction

Part I

The Microeconomics of the Business Network

Part II

The Behavioral Economics of Business and Social Networks

Chapter 6

The Affective Network

97

Network Heaven. Network Hell. Nature throwing us a curve. Incentive Motivation. Dopamine. The curious case of Benjamin Button's factory. The curious-er case of Benjamin Button's sales force. Distraction. Cold Calls. Toxic Information. Information overload overloaded. Inattention. Stress. The Cinderella Effect. Stress and Seawater. Network Hygiene.

Chapter 7

127

Game of Networks

The Knob of Motivation. Gamification. Gamification Gamed. Gamified Business Networks.

Introduction

Sales is the oldest profession, but whether you are selling yourself literally or figuratively, getting in front of the customer is often a major effort and the prime consumer of your time, and is generally thought of as a matter of persistence, not technique. For complex selling, prospective clients often have hardly the time or interest to attend to your value proposition. Thus, to get in front of them, you need more than a cold call, brochure, mailer, or advertising spot. You need an introduction. Often a satisfied customer will suffice, and 'word of mouth' can carry you forward to sales success. More often however, you rely on an informal network of colleagues outside of your company to introduce or refer you to prospective clients. You need in other words a business network. Business networks come in many forms, and whether they are embodied in your local Chamber of Commerce, Rotary club, trade groups, or even you and a colleague talking over a beer, these social networks seem subject to different sorts of rules as compared to the economic networks that drive business.

But they are not.

Business networks merely trade on another form of currency, namely information, yet this information economy is also rule based, and we will succeed or fail in sales depending on how we understand and implement these rules. The problem is that the rules of an information network are subtle, uncertain in prospect, and truth be told, cut against the grain of what we commonly believe our economic and human natures are like. From Dale Carnegie to Stephen Covey, the literature of sales and salesmanship attribute the success of informal business networks to the application of human virtue, the summoned motives that represent the best of us.

But economics is not built upon our better but our practical selves, and economies are not run on human virtue, but human self-interest. A core argument of this book is that the informal economies as represented by networking are no different. If humans at root are practical if not virtuous sorts, we will trace the subtle rules that govern how we trade information to meet practical ends. This is a marketplace where value is denominated informally, and gains value through knowledge, explanation, and their uses to persuade. It is the world of the salesperson.

For salespeople to be successful, they must first participate in and construct a marketplace that allows them to bring their ideas to the thoughtful consideration of others. This is not easy, and requires them to raise their perspective from viewing business networking as an art form to business networking as a science. However, science is far removed from the comfortable certitudes of the sales practitioner. The science of the business network requires explanations that evolve through questioning, challenge, and constant test. Following the scientist's axiom of disciplined self-doubt, there are thus no certitudes in this book, only observations that will sharpen, change, and perhaps improve on what we know. An explanation of the business network and how to design, control, and use it to further the success of the sales professional is the focus of this book. However, good explanations are deep things and must be informed and complemented by equally good explanations of not only the psychology of sales, but the psychology of motivation. This book is thus very different from business books that superficially describe networking and the sales process. I intend to show how business networking and the psychology of sales derives from first principles: the primary metaphors that describe how our minds work. Much of this book is the product of my experience both in success and failure as a sales professional, and the hard-won lessons of economics and psychology. Much of what I will say may be right, and much may be wrong, and all the better for a questioning attitude that I trust the reader will bring along as she reads this book.

The scope and purpose of this book

In the popular literature of sales and networking, success depends upon sharing knowledge and imparting the passion to succeed. Thus, appeals are made to the rational and emotional actors in all of us. Often one does not know when the reasoning stops and the emotion starts, as our rational and emotional interests are often invoked simultaneously in the logical and inspiring screed of those popular writers and pundits who want us to succeed while at the same time separating us from our dollars. Passing from self-help to academic knowledge, to make sense of our public and private worlds, reason and emotion are commonly moved to separate spheres, and so it goes in philosophy, psychology, and especially in economics. In this book, I follow the same outline, and address why it is *wrong*. It is argued that emotion and logic must always be addressed as interdependent and not separate entities in the proper design of business networks, just as they are for best practices in sales. However, it is my position that motivation comes from testable explanations of behavior, not the huckster's un-refutable emotional appeal that sadly infects much of the literature on sales and business networking today.

In part one, business networks are described as rational economic institutions, where information is traded for information following the rules of barter and monetary economies. Business networks facilitate transactions between individuals to further their economic interests, and to succeed business networks must be viewed as economic and not just social institutions. How these networks are structured influences greatly their success for the individuals involved. Various types of networks are discussed, along with the procedural keys to their success, and how and why the psychology of sales and sales success is utterly dependent upon proper networking skills.

In part two, business networks are described as economic institutions that succeed or fail dependent upon how they elicit *irrational* behavior in their members. This 'behavioral' economic perspective examines how human emotion or 'affect' is expectedly or unexpectedly elicited by business and social networks to either facilitate or impair productive behavior. To be effective, all networks must be 'affective', and from an overview of effective networks from past and present, it is demonstrated that the difference between average and superlative performance is dependent upon very subtle yet concrete aspects of network design, and how they engineer the literal passion to succeed. Finally, the conventional wisdom of business networking is contrasted and critiqued in light of our previous arguments, and the future of networking as well as its startling possibilities are discussed.

Part I

The Microeconomics of the Business Network

Chapter 1

The Business Network

Pitch Perfect

Sales is like baseball. You just get in front of a customer and make a pitch. Except for the fact that the value of striking out and hitting it out of the ballpark are reversed, it is a fine prospect overall. Sales is just a game of pitch and catch. In general, sales training, whether in a course, book, or lecture are all about coaching you to make that right pitch that connects to the customer. The problem is, potential customers are not as accommodating as the opposing player in the batter's box. Indeed, they would more often avoid you than show up on time, eager to listen to your pitch. So the salesperson, like a bush league pitcher, ends up spending his time chasing the customer. Unlike the pitch, the chase is not about perfecting the motions, but rather about making the motions. It is all about perspiration, not inspiration. The successful salesperson invariably exhausts himself cold calling, door knocking, and pleading to whomever would give him a second's listen. Along the way, he is motivated to stay the course by the inspiring screed of a self-help book or speaker, the positive lure of a commission, and a looming quota dangling over his head like the sword of Damocles.

Unlike marketing, sales and salesmanship is a topic that is scarcely remarked upon by an academic curriculum, and it is easy to see why. After all, incessantly beating the bushes or your head against the customer's door does not lend itself to academic philosophy. And so it goes, as sales books are oddly detached from academic sources that couldn't care less. Check out any popular sales book, and arguments are unreferenced, and are as ungrounded to the facts as an infomercial on vitamins. How to make the perfect pitch remains the focus. How do you to get in front of the perfect customer? Just be prepared to sweat.

But what if 'sweat' wasn't the issue, and indeed never was the issue? The source of this claim comes from an understanding of the information exchanges or networks that broker that information to the benefit of salesperson and client alike. That social networks are core to the sales process is hardly a revolutionary assumption, but as I will demonstrate in this book, we cannot suitably *explain* what makes social networks effective in the act of selling, and in the large, the art of persuasion. With a proper explanation, it will be argued that we must change how we sell by expanding our client conversation to include the complementary interests of our sales partners. This is an ironic proposition, since business networking is a topic alien to most books on selling. Yet a good explanation will allow us to test our proposition and demonstrate it to be true. With proper explanation, we can fine-tune our social networks to maximize their value to our clients and us. To arrive at a good explanation, we begin with a tale of the worst sales manager that ever was, namely you.

The World's Worst Sales Manager

You are a new sales manager, and a bad one, although you inexplicably think otherwise. Your sales team, eager to get started, gets five minutes of training on your complex IT, telephony, legal, etc. solution. When they are in front of the customer, you instruct them to talk sports, politics, or other assorted small talk, and the customer may (you hope) spontaneously bring up a need that fits your solution. The salesperson may perhaps ask a client a question about whether they are in the market for your solution, and then it is back to small talk. If the salesperson relays to you that the client does want to talk about your solution, you thank the salesperson for the effort and the lead, and promise them a just reward, someday. To you, sales is all about the kindness of strangers, and to fully benefit from business network, you need merely *appear* in a business network. If you appear often enough, our kindly human nature will take its course, and in a spate of mutual referrals, all will prosper.

Of course, you would be wrong.

Now let us alter our example a little. You are a salesperson who sells equally complex solutions, and you have a business network of sales colleagues who market complementary products and services to hundreds of clients that you would also like to meet. They know a bit about your services, maybe five minutes worth, and they too will visit many clients, full of sales conversations that represent your interest as much as small talk about baseball. Of course, if the customer mentions something that pertains to your interest, you will hear about it, maybe. And what does the referrer get in return, a cross referral, maybe.

The lesson from this example is simple. If a sales manager lightly manages his sales force, non-productivity is not just expected, it is assured. However, light management is standard issue for the sales colleagues who could if they chose qualify and secure referrals from their own client base. The question is, how can you manage a sales force whose allegiance is not to you. In other words, how can you manage the art of a *lateral sales manager*?

The Lateral Sales Manager

A vertical sales manager's job is easy to describe. The sales manager educates, motivates, and coaches a staff of sales professionals who are contractually bound to call, meet, present, support, and *sell* to current and prospective clients, all the while staying current on the products and services they sell. To ensure that their behavior at least trends in the right direction, the *contract* is the key. Behave well, and salary, commission, and your job security is secure. Fail to do so, and it is all in jeopardy.

A lateral sales manager on the other hand lightly manages or 'networks' with a group of peer sales professionals who sell complementary products and services. It is implicitly understood that his peers would keep their ears open for opportunities and perhaps ask a question or two that would reflect his interests. In return, you promise a referral in exchange. Too often, it doesn't work that way. Qualified referrals remain hard to come by, and you end up spinning your wheels in endless networking meetings that are spun to you as the portal to sales success.

But why do some business networks work and some don't, and how can you know the difference in advance, and change the one's you are in to make them more effective? To arrive at an answer, we must first define what a business network is.

A business network is a barter economy where information rather than money is the medium of exchange, and indirectly leads to sales. Information is 'traded' between individual business partners. This information in turn is provided to their clients who will express an interest in learning more. The partners then make cross referrals of their clients, and thus gain access to them pursuant to a meeting, proposal, and an eventual sale. This concept is simple in theory, and underscores every business network from a simple pairing of sales professionals over coffee to a networking function hosting hundreds.

The Social Network

In contrast to a business network, a social network reflects a social economy where information is traded that is weakly related or unrelated to sales. This information may involve personal, professional, or technical knowledge, such as fishing clubs, chess clubs, church groups, or groups of computer professionals. For example, an accountant may join the local chapter of the AICPA, and in social gatherings of his colleagues' share or trade information about best practices, new regulations, etc. These groups also share generic interests as well, as that accountant you meet may want to discuss the computer services you may provide which may lead to a sale.

As we will note in chapter 9 of this book, a common element among contemporary definitions of business networking is that effective business networking is a byproduct of effective social networking. Build a reputation for likeability, trustworthiness, and expert status, and people will find you out, just as you find out where you can buy a Coke or Car Insurance by virtue of repeated simplistic advertising. Like building a brand by endlessly repeating a catchy slogan, if you hang around enough, people may just 'brand' you. This passive approach to sales or 'weak' business networking works if you have the time, but most of us don't. An active approach to using networking to gain sales must cut radically to the chase, just as it must do when a salesperson begins her day. Although social networking is an excellent adjunct to business networking, the latter to be successful must be entirely focused from the outset on sales.

The concept of the barter economy is rooted in microeconomic theory, and attributes behavior not to intrinsic self-caused motivations, but rather extrinsic incentives that are facilitated by economic institutions. Thus, a market economy motivates better than a command economy because the former provides the intellectual scaffolding for flexible incentives. However, what are the essential structural elements that make a barter economy work? To understand this let us consider an example not from the business world, but from an agrarian one.

What is Microeconomics?

Microeconomics: The trading of goods and services or the illusion thereof for money or illusions that will never lead to money. Microeconomics demonstrates that by trading one illusion for another more profitable illusion, one can be rich and flat broke at the same time.

In these troubled economic times, the big economic picture is all that counts, and good times and bad have all the accuracy of a long term weather forecast, which is not much. Economics seems far removed from our daily affairs because it's simply not local. To gain predictive power if not foresight into the big picture, locality is everything, and microeconomics is key.

Microeconomics is a branch of economics that studies how individuals allot their time, money, and other limited resources in exchange for other goods both material and immaterial. Normally, it applies to local markets where goods and services are traded for currency. Open a grocery store or restaurant and you are immersed at once in a micro-economic environment.

Currency is simply a generalized token or reward that you can trade for anything. In marketplaces, money is traded for tangible products, yet there is another means of exchange that occurs that involves not currency, but the coin of individual and collective opinion that indirectly monetizes information. For example, a new painting you completed, the novel you just finished, or that bunch of tomatoes you just harvested are tradable in marketplaces that assign real values to the goods you wish to trade. Thus, the painting is off to the art gallery, the novel is out to the bookstore, and the tomatoes are sent to the farmer's market, and all are offered in exchange for currency. But the artist can also be 'paid' in the approval of an art critic, the writer by a favorable book review, and the farmer by a blue ribbon. This information, denoted in the tokens of formalized regard increase the likelihood that people will actually purchase our wares, and we often feel we can defer receiving actual compensation in consideration of a bit of good 'press' today. Indeed, human motivation is remarkable because incentives often defer actual monetary compensation that may or will never occur, so that individuals may trade in a virtual currency of mutual regard with eventual tangible compensation as unreachable as a mirage.

As the tokens in our new digital economy become virtualized and we progressively 'buy in' to this, then badges, ribbon, likes, nudges, and the like become the coin of a new economy, and with this digital age people become motivated not by the reality but by its reflected image. This is represented in an internet reality that establishes new marketplaces that are far removed from those human marketplaces that involve real people abutting each other with ideas and wares. For new age technological pundits, virtual marketplaces are the wave of the future, and this would certainly seem to be the case as commerce moves from the marketplace on the ground to a marketplace in the cloud.

Can microeconomics shed some light on this trend? It ultimately depends upon how an understanding of virtual incentives motivate, and the best way to do so is by knowing how they work in human social networks, and on a personal level, how the quality and timing of extrinsic incentives motivate the organic and not metaphorical human mind. Ironically, as we shall see, virtual incentives can accentuate the importance of the face-to-face networks they purport to replace.

Down on the Farm

Consider three farmers: Bob, who grows pumpkins; Tom, who grows grapes; and Danielle, who grows apples. They meet every week, and since times are tough and money is tight, their currency is denominated in the foodstuffs they grow. Let's say that Bob successfully touts the excellence of his pumpkins to Tom, and recipes in hand shows they may be fashioned into pies, tarts, and Halloween lanterns. Suitably impressed, Tom takes several. Bob however has no need for Tom's grapes, but he does need Danielle's apples, and straightaway gets a clutch of apples from Danielle after she also shows him how to prepare apples into delicious treats. For his part, Danielle wants some of Tom's grapes, and learning from Tom how to make grape juice and wine from the fruit, grabs a dozen bunches. Tom duly records how much produce have been exchanged that day between all three farmers, and the group agrees to meet the following week to trade again.

In summary, Bob gives pumpkins to Tom, and Tom give grapes to Danielle, and Danielle gives apples to Bob. Tom records who gave what to who, how much was given and received, and from past exchanges charts the future obligation of each farmer. Thus, if Tom is giving far more of his grapes to the other partners than he is receiving in produce, the others would 'owe' him the balance.

The Original Business Network

This example demonstrates how three otherwise broke farmers can create a barter economy that benefits all of them even though no money changes hands. The requirements for such an economy are simple: a place or venue in a congenial environment where they can meet with their wares, a strong interest in the complementary wares of each other due to familiarity (seeing the pumpkin, grapes, apples) and education (learning how to prepare the pumpkin, grapes, apples), and a token economy that provides the measure of who gave what to who. For the latter, the 'token' may be a means of exchange such as money, or in the case of our example public record of what has been exchanged. If any of these requirements are altered or removed, the value of the network may decline or be eliminated. For example, if the farmers have no knowledge of when and where they are to meet or meet in a distractive environment, have little interest in each other's products, and have no means of measuring who is giving what to whom, the network becomes markedly less useful or becomes useless.

For market economies, whether reliant upon money or barter, these principles are implicit and clear. However, for contemporary barter economies wherein information is traded, this is surprisingly not the case. Indeed, for the market for information, a quasi-barter economy is often the settled standard, but it is not a standard that is well understood. As an example, consider three salespeople: a guy who sells voice (telephony) systems (Bob), an guy who sells information systems (Tom), and a gal who sells wireless infrastructure (Danielle) that all this runs on. Each of them sells their prospective services to an established and prospective client base numbering in the hundreds, and each naturally would be delighted if their colleagues would refer them clients from their own customer base.

As a network of acquaintances, they can obviously barter information or leads with one another, but they do not. The reason they do not is due to defects in their implicit barter economy. Primarily, the problem is that each of the three salespeople may meet with each other separately from time to time, but not as a group. Secondly, although their interests are complementary, their professional interest is not strong because they are invariably not educated on the capabilities of each other's services and how they may serve their clients. Third, even if they were to refer to one another, they have no way of measuring what they have referred and to whom. The result is that each of them find it hard to meet, hard to refer, and hard to account for their exchange of referrals.

To redress this situation, our sales people may wish to improve upon or supplement their network by joining a networking group. Ranging from the Rotary to the Chamber to the local PTA, networking groups are uniform in their implicit promise, but their deliverables are hampered not by the personal skills of the individual in networking, but from disincentives deriving from their structure as barter economies. This is a critical point, as the literature on networking generally argues; the benefit of such groups is dependent upon individual sales skills, personal character, and persistence that are independent of the structure of the group. Thus, to be a successful networker in your local Rotary, Chamber, or PTA, mutual obligations that lead to referrals are due to personal virtues, and far less owing to the structure of these groups as incipient barter economies and how those economies structure incentive. In short, the value of a business network is commonly viewed as standing apart from the market dynamics of a network, and our success emerges instead from the *psycho*-dynamics of human motivation that are manipulated independent *of* the network.

For our three salespeople, their performance is also measured against this psychodynamic principle, and success or failure in business networking is a measure of their individual sufferance with professional networks that incompletely serve their needs. Of course, the Rotary, Chamber, and PTA would beg to differ, and continue to extol their excellence as exemplars of how business networks should be run. In the following chapter, I will attempt to prove them wrong.

Chapter 2

Networks to Know, Love, and Dread

Bob, Tom and Danielle go Network Shopping

Eager to meet with other folks who could help them expand their sales contacts and leads, Bob, Tom and Danielle individually go shopping for the perfect network. As colleagues who have met each other from time to time, they are already members of many networks. Besides their tenuous ties of acquaintance, they are invariably networked with clients, friends, like-minded professionals, and vendors, and meet them formally or informally in face-to-face settings, or virtually through phone calls, emails, and the nudges, likes, and pokes of social media. The problem our trio faces is deciding which types of networks best repay the investment of their valuable time, and how to use them to maximize their effectiveness. Specifically, what rules can they employ to predict which network serves their needs best, and how can they best use these networks to further their business success?

The main criteria they must consider are the primary and secondary benefits of joining a social network. If a member of our trio were to join the local chapter of Toastmasters, the Rotary Club, or the Chamber of Commerce, do the primary functions of these groups (public speaking, community service, or business lobbying) complement their value as sources of business referrals? Assuming that they do not, then the benefits of public speaking, community service, or lobbying are transformed into the direct costs of gaining potential referrals. Thus, our threesome must work within these limitations. These limitations are nothing less than how these groups, shorn of their explicit purpose, meet their *implicit* purpose as judged as business networks. Whether primary or secondary to the group, this purpose is compared against a micro-economic standard that reflects how well it meets the criteria of a barter economy of information. To this end, we will consider ten different types of business networks that comprise a salesperson and his clients, vendors, interests, and peers. We will also examine 'for profit' networks as well as networks within networks. All of them will be judged by how they match the economic requirements of a business network, and our behavior within them will be accounted for and predicted by the incentives both explicit and implicit that are created and facilitated by how these networks are structured. We will begin with a network that many salespeople participate in by well, not networking at all.

The Outsourced Network

The sales person is paid to sell, and may consider lead generation to be either beneath him or the province of the marketing department of the company. There is no need for networking because networking is done through the adept use of advertising, social media, cold calling, word of mouth, etc. that is performed by your marketing and not sales department. The salesperson is as dependent upon a lead stream as the hapless real estate salesmen in the play Glengarry Glenross, with hopefully all performers bad or good sharing in the bounty. Because the salesperson does not own lead generation, he cannot secure leads through trading information he already has. Thus an outsourced network is not a business network. Having a source of readymade leads is a nice job if you can get it, but unfortunately most sales people have to secure their own leads themselves, and their first and invariably bumbling attempt at this represents their first network, or a network of acquaintances.

The Acquaintance Network

The acquaintance network is our default network of choice. In fact, it is overwhelmingly so. Indeed, the sum of active participants across all other business networks is but a small fraction of those who could participate. For those who consistently participate, the number is even less. However, for the acquaintance network, everybody participates, in a fashion. What is an acquaintance network? The acquaintance network represents you as a salesperson networking without understanding, procedure or plan with individuals who are less than colleagues, and are mere acquaintances. You don't participate in business networks as much as bump into them. You may go to a Chamber function once or twice, talk to vendors now and then, and even ask a client for a referral from time to time. Your involvement in and understanding of networks is limited, and you dabble rather than commit to any information marketplace. The reason for your ambivalence is simple, you simply don't understand them, and without a proper explanation, all you can go by are the lessons of experience, which generally don't speak to success. Indeed, they speak instead to the orneriness of human behavior that is due to motives inscrutable and confusing. Because you don't understand how networks work you don't know how to 'work' them or modify their structural weaknesses into strengths, and you tend to attribute the disinterest of the parties serving your interest to personal variables that are out of your control, or the veritable unkindness of strangers.

However, the real reason for our fleeting interest in networking is that their motivating structure as marketplaces is subordinated to often-ungrounded assumptions of the individual motivations of its members. The reason why clients or colleagues do not give you referrals is due to intrinsic aspects of personal character and not the lack of extrinsic incentive. Personal motives are inscrutable, are either right or wrong, and are reinforced by complement or reduced by disdain. On the other hand, behavior guided by incentive is clear, simple, and always 'right', not in terms of its intrinsic value but because of psychological necessity.

For example, consider a person who continually and literally bumps into you. If you didn't know that he couldn't see you because he was visually impaired, then it's easy to ascribe fault rather than necessity to his behavior. If he were at fault, you would 'correct' his behavior through disparagement or avoidance. If his behavior were however out of necessity, then you would hand him a pair of glasses and perhaps get to know him better. Similarly, for human behavior, behavior is always right, and understanding is repaid immeasurably through the corrective measures we can take to correct our faulty vision.

If one person understands the behavior of business networks, or better, if many people gain that same understanding, then subtle motives become concrete ones, and like a motivation inferred by Sherlock Holmes, we are all in on the solution. For our experience with business networks and its many variations, we need to know what to expect and be able to predict how people will behave merely by noting the subtle ways networking groups arrange incentives. Of all networking groups, incentives are most clear and certain from the client network.

The Client Network

The easiest, most obvious and most dependable source of business referrals represents the clients you and your company already have. Since they are presumably pleased with your service, they are a natural source of referrals both solicited and unsolicited. It is always pleasant to receive a referral from a client who notices an opportunity to present to you from his own circle of professional contacts. The referral may only be a given name or names of colleagues who he may tell you to call and mention his recommendation, or he may call them himself and recommend them personally to you. The latter of course is the best way of securing a referral appointment, since your client trades off his relationship with his colleague to gain you an appointment. Whether he does so or not depends in large measure on his sense of obligation to you. If you have served him above the level of service he expects, you can trade upon that relationship and have him advocate for you on request, and you will feel confident that he will endorse you when his colleagues express a need for your services.

The problem with a client network is that your client may not have many colleagues he knows well enough to comfortably refer you to, may not fully understand the services you offer, and will rarely advocate on your behalf to the customers and colleagues he has because there is frankly little he will expect in exchange. In other words, even though you may meet with him often, your interests are generally not complementary, he is not trained in your offerings to represent them adequately, and there is little incentive for him to actively and consistently seek our referrals for you. Although he can provide some knowledge of your skills to a colleague and make recommendations from time to time, it is often difficult for you to return the favor. Nonetheless, in spite of its limitations, a client network is the default network for many companies, as 'word of mouth' can grow a company even if the referrer receives nothing in exchange, and even if the salesperson does nothing at all.

The Tale of the Idle Woodsman

Referrals from a client network are often critical to judging a salesperson's production, but not necessarily in judging a salesperson's performance. This is because sales rarely follow within days of a salesperson's activity, but can occur weeks and even years afterwards. With that delay comes uncertainty of the degree of contingency between the salesperson's performance and the sale, so that an eventual sale may or may not be due to a salesperson's effort. This is often a cause of great envy, dissatisfaction, and conflict within a sales force, and often results in the reward to a salesperson for sales success and penalty for poor performance simultaneously. Unfortunately, sales success is too often seen as a better measure of a salesperson's quality than poor performance to top management. After all, making quota doesn't lie, or does it?

Consider for example a woodsman who can almost cut down trees. Because of the peculiar hard to cut nature of our hypothetical forest, he hacks at one after another, and gets most of them to lean or get at least a bit shaky. After he chops on a thousand or so trees in his designated acreage or territory, he sits back and waits for nature to take its course. Many of the hacked trees will eventually fall, and many un-chopped trees as well. As time goes on, the causes for their falling multiplies as termites, old age, disease, combined with or acting separately from the woodsman's effort may be the cause. Furthermore, the specific contribution of each also becomes more uncertain. What is certain however it that the woodsman is a reliable producer. If he has a quota of trees to bring to market from his territory, he can easily make it by just standing around while nature takes its course. He is making quota by merely 'taking orders' when each tree falls, and when the woodsman retires, he may be replaced by the favored nephew of the landowner, who will promptly make quota by just surveying which trees have fallen.

This would not go unnoticed by a newly hired woodsman who can be chopping like a lumberman possessed, and has great performance but marginal production. The mismatch is evident to the new woodsman, and her envy of her more productive colleague is real and deserved. However, since the new woodsman is chopping her trees deep in the forest, the landowner does not know if this lack of performance is due a lack of good chopping skills or simply a lack of time to bring the woodsman's efforts to fruition. So he may give the woodsman time to produce, or 'axe' the woodsman's job, seeing the fact that she had not made quota overrules the best effort that she only reported.

The key argument is this example as applied to salespeople is that lagging indicators of performance are much easier to determine than leading indicators. A leading indicator of course predicts the future, but a lagging indicator predicts the past. It is in other words easy to reward production but not performance because what is determined to be a good performance or effort is uncertain. Whereas the trees hide the new woodsman's performance, the salesperson's performance is hidden in the unknowable forest of cold calls and client meetings. Because the sales manager cannot easily measure the quality of the salesperson's effort, he often depends instead on the quantity of the salesperson's results rather than the quality of her effort. The problem is that by rewarding production rather than performance, the sales manager does not directly reward effort, and because of this cannot shape the performance of his sales team to meet and surpass the long-term goals of the enterprise. The remedy for this problem is to define what best effort is, or what once in front of a client the best approach is to pursue and make a sale. That reflects not business networking, but as we shall later see, the science of salesmanship.

The client network is a passive resource for the salesperson because he is not actively exchanging one good, namely a client referral, for another. Indeed, he may often not receive due credit or he may be over credited for a client referral since it is so uncertainly connected to his own efforts. Depending upon the perspective of management, making quota through client referrals may make the salesperson the hero or the goat, or more commonly somewhere in between. The client network, in spite of its value, does not separate the salesperson from his peers because he cannot use it to distinguish himself through the exchange or barter of information. It may from time to time distinguish him, particularly if a good lead or leads come from his clients, but this is more likely due to accident rather than design. On the other hand, networking groups that rely upon mutual social or professional interest give credit to the salesperson, yet are less well understood and often far less reliable in the production of leads.

Interest Networks

An interest network trades in the exchange of non-business information that does not result in sales, with business networking of only secondary value. Special interest networks such a charitable, religious, and social groups are common, and the Toastmasters, or Church Men's Club or local PTA are only a few of the score of interest networks we can join and participate in. These groups appeal to the specific and generic interests of its members. For example, a member of your Church Men's Club shares your interest in spiritual affairs, but can also discuss with you the vagaries of tax law, which can lead to him doing your taxes, for a fee of course. Nonetheless, the problem is that these groups primary interest can obscure and hinder your sales interest, as the other members do not primarily want to know what you do or how to help you do what you do. In addition, the number of members in interest groups may have little turnover or are small, so you experience diminishing returns once you get to know their current membership. Nonetheless, if you find value in the primary offerings of these groups, then they can be of value for the infrequent referrals your group colleagues may provide. However, if you look at your time as an investment rather than a donation, professional networks are a much better alternative.

Professional Networks

In contrast to interest networks, a professional network trades in the exchange of business related information. Like an interest network, much of this information is unrelated to increasing sales, but to increasing indirect benefits to the enterprise such as education (trade groups), lobbying (Chambers of Commerce), or charitable work (Rotary Club). Professional networks such as the Chamber of Commerce may also appeal to the generic interest of its members, such as providing a venue where members from different professions may meet to network. However, this is a function duplicated by interest networks as well, and because of its commonality is a far less compelling reason to join a professional network.

Professional networks often advertise business networking as secondary to their purpose if they occur at all, and if offered these business networking events act as a 'walled garden' that is set up expressly for that purpose. For Chambers of Commerce monthly or bi-weekly networking events or business socials are attended primarily by sales professionals or sales minded executives in setting that are more akin to a singles bar or club that a bonafide marketplace. Like a singles bar, 'deals' can be struck up and consummated with a sales call and perhaps a sale. For example, a sales rep for an IT company may meet the COO of a distribution company that needs computer services and arrange a future meeting on the spot. For the rest, the hope is that the exchange of business cards will result in future business, a hope unfortunately that is generally not realized. The problem of course with making brief contacts among disinterested parties is that unlike a fine wine, their interest does not mature in time. They will be far more likely to forget you than remember you in time of need because they will likely personally never meet you again. To get them to remember your services, you need to network better, and a better network experience is something a professional network can only begin to provide.

Overall, networking meetings in professional networks break the fundamental principles of an information exchange, and thus sharply reduce their benefits. In the fluid and noisy confines of a networking meeting, it is difficult to sort out, reach out, or talk to someone who has complementary interest. Even if a meeting occurs, one often does not have the time or means to trade or mark the trade of information, and one is unsure when he will meet that contact again. There is a simple solution to such a problem, namely invite your contact to some place where you can network in private. However, for private networking to succeed, the business social must first be designed properly.

Running in Circles

A quick glance of the membership directory of any professional network reveals a mismatch between who is participating in the network and who is a member of that network. Read the member list of any local Chamber of Commerce, and you will discover captains of industry, civic leaders, and successful entrepreneurs. Go to a chamber-networking group and you are more likely to meet Bobbi, the owner of a doggy hotel or Toni, the reseller of scented candles. So why the disinterest among all those top professionals who need to get out once in a while for a little fresh air and professional networking? Are they being callous, overworked, or just indifferent? Or could it be the doggy lady?

It's the doggy lady. Top-level executives don't want to meet the doggy lady, and chances are they don't want to meet you either. But this doesn't mean that they don't want to network. The degree of network participation from members is low in professional networks because of the egalitarian philosophy of those networks. In short, a networking circle is presumed to be one size fits all and encompasses all social circles. However, this is not true. People run in certain social circles not only because of a commonality of interests, but because the mutual benefits exchanged are likely to be comparable. Returning to our example of our farmer's market trio of Rob, Tom, and Danielle, the person who is head of a pumpkin agribusiness does not want to meet individual farmers of grapes and apples, even though those farmers may want to meet him. He would rather instead network with the owner of a winery or a nationwide apple pie bakery. Similarly, a bank president, head of a medical clinic, corporate sales manager, or law firm partner certainly wants to network to sell their services, but only among similar peers who can bring equally much to the table. Like a high stakes poker game, you get to play for high stakes only is you have high stakes to offer.

Ultimately, all networks are stratified not only by personal and professional interests but also the equivalence of the mutual incentives each party may give. Professional networks assume that members share an egalitarian view towards each other because of the unifying purpose of the network, but networks serve multiple purposes that embody different incentives for behavior. Hence, a professional network can differentiate itself into multiple networks not because of who the members are but what they have to offer. However, because the administrators of professional networks don't understand that different social circles run within networking circles, it is understandable that they would be confused that most members when faced with a homogenous networking event elect to stay at home.

Sins of a Professional Network

Professional networks stress the value of its social events, so they therefore can still run a pretty good networking social, right? Well, it depends. Too often, the view seems to be that socializing occurs by a sort of interpersonal osmosis, where our interests blend in, and we leave personally enriched and full of leads. Thus, it doesn't matter if the event is at an inconvenient location, has bad acoustics and mediocre food, and that you don't have a clue who all those people are in that big meeting room.

Venue for your next business social

Far Away Location: *The meeting is held across the dark forest, beyond the misty mountains, past the desert of despair, and you have to pay for parking.*

Strange Venue: *The meeting place is at a men's store (you talk to the mannequins), storage facility (like meeting in a missile silo or rail car), or car dealership (watch where you put your coffee cup please!)*

No Introductions: *You mingle with two hundred people who don't know who is who, and as nobody is hosting the thing to introduce you, a networking meeting inseparable from a congregation of strangers waiting for the train.*

Unappealing Crowd: *Everyone you meet is a lower level clerk, sales trainee, or reseller of scented candles.*

The Business Social

Professional networks frequently arrange socializing events, are clear about the general purpose of socializing (making friends, getting leads), yet misunderstand how etiquette gets in the way *of* socializing, and what to do afterwards. Etiquette? Indeed, politeness can easily impede meeting whom you want to meet, and avoiding those you don't. Unless you are a sociopath or snake oil salesman, you will be exceedingly polite and a bit anxious about the whole thing, and to the detriment of your business success.

To illustrate this predicament, let's say that you just joined a professional network, and attend your first business social. You will see a room full of people chatting amicably. Often they will have no nametag, so you don't know who is who. Even if they did, no one is there to take you around the group, introducing you to people you may want to meet. You must do that yourself. But that requires a bit of boldness in meeting people and interjecting yourself between people who are talking, and that could be rude. And even if you do that, and happen to meet a bunch of folks of complementary interests who can share with you business intelligence and leads, you leave with business cards and polite thank you's, and have a lonely wait by the phone for them to call you, for to call them and ask for a meeting might be rude. But let's say again that you give them a call and suggest a meeting to discuss sharing what you do and what you could do for each other as well as each other's clients. You meet once, chat amicably and with mutual interest, and never meet one another again. That is because you may not have the time, and besides, to suggest another meeting could be rude. Then of course is the problem of having to deal with people that want to meet, call, and sell you stuff, and you would rather have nothing to do with them or their wares. However, to just say no may be rude.

Etiquette denotes the subtle rules of interpersonal behavior for a given social setting that are mutually understood and agreed. If you are looking for your networking experience to be productive for your time while minding the proprieties of etiquette, it will be far more so if the business social occurs with proper introductions, identifications, and perhaps a pre-screening of attendees. Nonetheless, etiquette does demand that you extend common courtesies to folks who you would rather not meet. That is true in any business or social network. However, professional networks ultimately succeed or fail through the private networks they incubate from business socials and the rules that they outline *for* those private networks. To be a successful member of a professional network, you must therefore understand the rules of how such private networks work. Similarly, for a professional network to succeed and grow, it must be able to provide the right social setting wherein private networks may be cultivated. By understanding and accepting their unique rules, then its members can successfully play by them for their own benefit and that of the larger group, and above all never seem rude.

To understand why mutually agreed rules for private networks are critical, consider a personal example. If you are a single person looking for a mate, singles networks are necessary for the creation of private networks, those one to one relationships that lead to marriage. However, if you don't know the rules of dating or if no one teaches you the rules, a singles network is of far less value as all your budding relationships will fail. Similarly, business socials are necessary for the creation of private networks where true business occurs. The private network represents multiple meetings wherein both individuals trade business information or referrals that lead to sales. Unlike dating, the rules governing private networks are unclear. Because people don't understand private networks and how they should work, professional networks are bound to be far less successful or even fail. So how do private networks and their variants work?

Network Mashups

In our farmer's market, Bob, Tom, and Danielle are perfectly content to trade their produce, but networks can trade in other things as well. For example, Bob may not need the produce of his network partners, but he may seek only information about how to grow his crop better, whereas Tom may only want to hang around his partners to socialize because this is one of the few times that he can catch-up with his neighbors in a short period of time. Only Danielle may want to trade her produce with the others, but is disappointed when they are focused on other goals during the networking event. The challenge for each of the dissatisfied partners is for them to find other partners who want to network about the things they want to commonly trade. However, as we will see, this is easier said than done.

People participate in networks to trade particular things, whether it is goods, services, or just social or business information. If they mix them up you have a network 'mashup' or blend of two or more different networking aims, with different people congregating to trade entirely different things.

Nowhere is this more apparent than in the 'After hour's' Business Socials hosted by the Chamber of Commerce or other professional organizations. Go to a business social and you will find people who are there to: a) socialize, b) network with other peers, c) obtain information on how to run their company better, or

d) just attend out of obligation to their corporate superiors. Each of these goals are unique (and largely incompatible), and mixing them up causes tensions as the social rules of the meeting are unclear. If you are there to network and sell your product, do you really want to stand around and listen to a colleague talk to you about politics or sports? Similarly, if you are there to get information about certain products and services that can help your company grow, do you want to hear a sales pitch instead, and be bothered afterwards by sales calls and unwanted email solicitations? Certainly, there may be those who are there to do all three, but for many others it is an unnecessary encumbrance in light of the simple solution.

What's wrong with this picture?[1]

The solution is to simply break the networks up, with after business socials expressly advertised as being solely for 1) socialization, 2) sales, or 3) information. The latter is particularly tricky, since providing product information or advice can easily morph into a sales opportunity that an individual may not invite. This can easily be addressed if the rules of an

---

[1] Not much networking, that's what. So, what are these folks up to? The lady on the left is being asked out by the guy on the right. The fellow with the red tie is talking about the upcoming NFL season, the lady in the white blouse is being pitched annuities by an insurance salesman, the lady in green is trading business cards with another lady as a preface for a later meeting where they can trade business leads, and the guy on the far right just wants to know the best way to cook lasagna.

information seminar are clear. At an Informational Networking Event, the Chamber could setup display tables for salespeople to display products and other information about their company. Additionally, the exhibitors can be forbidden from soliciting the business cards or other private data from the individuals they meet. This forces the salespeople to present their products, the associated value, and the buying triggers during the networking event to encourage qualified buyers to follow-up with the salesperson on the next business day, thus forcing salespeople to wait until called, and earning that call from the quality of the information they provide. Indeed, nothing would be more inviting than a row of kiosks that do not have fishbowls for cards, and with salespeople who are there to provide you with information and nothing more as you bask in your deserved anonymity. When buyers have valid information and control the buying decision, buyer's remorse is significantly reduced and repeat sales increase.

Private Networks

In a singles bar, you invite that great person you've met to go to a more quiet and private place to get to know them better. The same thing occurs when you meet someone who perhaps could be an excellent business partner or client. If the person you meet needs something you offer, then you set up an appointment to see him at their office, and after the sale they become part of your client network. On the other hand, if you have something to offer to his clients or each other's clients, your new relationship becomes a private network that is likely much more profitable. In other words, a private network may consist of an audience with a decision maker who as a gatekeeper represents many accounts and potential leads.

For example, you may meet a potential client who needs your services and propose a business relationship, or you may meet a potential client who can either resell or spread the word about your services to her client base. In the former case, you leverage that meeting into a sales proposal and hopefully a sale. In the latter case, if that client can resell your product to her clients or promote them to her customers, then you have the opportunity to exchange the value she provides for a commission or perhaps a reciprocal lead. Either way, reciprocity is the coin of the business relationship between you and your client who is now your partner.

As a business network, a private network represents a minimum of two individuals who trade referrals of clients who wish to learn more about and perhaps purchase the other's products or services. A real estate agent for example may refer her clients to an agent for a title company and vice versa, or a telephony firm may mutually trade leads with an IT system integrator. If they frequently meet to do this, then their complementary professional interests will result in the trade of information that is monetized by resulting prospective sales. Frequent follow up meetings are key, for without them a private network, like a single date between two individuals, will fail to develop into a true business relationship.

A private network is not limited to two individuals, and may expand to a group of parties who provide complementary goods and services. Thus, a real estate agent, builder, house inspector, banker, and title company may provide a circle of vendors who can provide value to each other and meet frequently to exchange referrals. In this case, the third element of a barter network, namely an ongoing record of who refers what to who, is critical to determine who is pulling their own weight and to maintain a sense of business equity.

A private business network in its most basic form represents vendors who *must* refer partners to clients in order to provide the latter demanded goods and services that they cannot or choose not to provide. Like a client network, oftentimes this referral network is passive, and a referral is relayed because the client has expressed a need to a vendor rather than that vendor discovering that need through an expansion of his normal client conversation. Although generally neglected, this expanded conversation is important for further sales opportunities, and may include aspects of needed products and services that the client is unaware or entirely new products and services that may be of benefit to the client. This latter function may entail growing the private network to include partners who may expand the products and services that a salesperson may discuss with or offer to a client.

A member of a private business network introduces other members of their group to their respective clients. She can also expand her contribution to the group and the number of individuals who can contribute to the group by expanding the number of his business partners, who as mutual gatekeepers may provide a source of expanded customer conversations that leads to more referrals and sales. In this way, a private network can grow into a group of gatekeepers or resellers that can provide a source of client introductions and sales opportunities that may be endless. This dynamic version of a private network is called a vendor network when money and goods are traded and a social VAR when information is traded with an indirect result in sales.

The Vendor Network

Whereas the client network is the default business network for all business people, the vendor network is nearly as universal, but generally fails as a business network. Many businesses represent and resell the products of vendors (e.g., car dealers, computer distributors, etc.), and add value to a vendor's product by knowing, installing, supporting, and advertising it better than the vendor could economically do on his own. The value added reseller or VAR adds value to the vendor's product, and the vendor provides value in turn by providing a superior product, pricing, support, and often leads. However, the vendor network is not intrinsically a business network because it does not primarily embody a barter economy. In other words, information is generally not traded between individuals within the vendor and reseller's organizations. For example, a VAR may sell a technology product offered by his vendor, but the vendor will generally not offer for trade any information about his clients and their needs to the VAR in return for similar information. The vendor may be aware of specific needs of its clients outside of its line of business that may be valuable to you, but it will rarely offer them to you in trade or otherwise because the relationship is constrained by the primary contractual relationship of vendor and reseller. Nonetheless, the vendor and VAR relationship can have the adjunct characteristics of a business network if they have supplemental skill and product sets that are more profitable if information about them is traded rather than resold. The often underestimated value of such a relationship requires a complete rethinking of the VAR relationship to incorporate the rules of trading or bartering information, and incorporates the positive attributes of the other business networks we discussed. This new type of networking arrangement we will call the Social VAR.

The Social VAR Network

A value-added reseller adds value to a product or service by explaining to the client how he uses it within his company, and how he as a reseller can add value to the sale through service and support. The VAR may also add value to a product that *it does not sell*. The question is how can a VAR monetize the value that is brought to the product or service and the resulting customer interest in purchasing it? In its simplest and most common form, the VAR may refer a client to a business partner without formally requesting any leads in exchange. If the partner reciprocates with a referral, then it is no more expected than a referral from a satisfied client, as in a client network. On the other hand, if the business partner is in the position to provide and expect referrals in exchange for referrals from his business partner, this creates the rudiments of a private network.

Private networks are distinguished from the social VAR because the former represent a quasi-barter or economic network, wherein certain key aspects of the network are undeveloped or missing not only because they are misunderstood, but because they are not *enforced*. To understand this, let us return to Bob, Tom, and Danielle. Individual members of the trio may turn up at the farmer's market only from time to time, learn only partly the benefits of each other's products (like that great recipe for pumpkin pie), and may only partially track the exchange of goods between members. To address these problems, the private network must be managed, or be subject to rules that are not only evident, but are enforced. Thus, each of our trio must regularly attend the farmer's market, know each other's products, and reliably record the exchange of products. If not, they face the penalty of expulsion from the group.

For any economy to function efficiently, its ground rules must be not only clear but also enforceable. This of course is the role of government, which sets standards for the representation of the reliability and quality of goods and services traded in economic environments as well as enforces the contracts that represent those transactions. For information economies such as client, professional, interest, and private networks, enforceable rules are absent governing the trade of information. Thus, if a client provides you with a referral, there is no enforceable rule that requires that you must do the same. A social VAR is different however because it enforces adherence to the rules of the group. A social VAR thus meets all the standards of an information barter network and optimizes them through enforceable rules. The members of a social VAR have strong complementary professional interests, meet frequently and at set times, use a token economy to track the trade of calls, referrals, and sales, and enforce the rules of the group as a condition of membership. The social VAR requires structure, but it also requires leadership to grow and maintain the group as well as and enforce its rules. Neither structure nor leadership are necessarily easy things to provide for an essentially not for profit organization, a void that can be filled if the members pay for these things by joining a 'for profit' social VAR.

The For Profit Social VAR

"It is difficult to get a man to understand something when his salary depends upon him not understanding it." Upton Sinclair.

In our example of a farmer's market, it is very easy for our three farmers Rob, Tom, and Danielle to set up a few stalls in an open space and start doing business with others and each other. Although the rules of running a successful farmer's market may be obvious to us, it certainly may not be obvious to our trio. So they were lucky that an aspiring entrepreneur set up a few inexpensive stalls, invited merchants including our trio of course to bring their wares, set up and enforced attendance and barter tracking rules, and charged an annual fee to all vendors for the right to participate in the market. Wanting to maximize his income for his enterprise that he was soon replicating across the land, our entrepreneur began to invite vendors who had wares that were not of complementary interest to our trio, like salespersons for time-shares and exercise clubs. Although that interfered with our trio communicating and trading with one another, that was Ok since they contributed to our entrepreneur's profit. Flush with success, our farmer's market tycoon would write a manual or two or three extolling the uniqueness of his enterprise and why all networking routes led to Rome, or in other words, his business networking empire.

Carried from illustration to reality, this example has its truest and most successful representation in the nationwide business network called Business Networking International. Founded by Ivan Misner in 1985, BNI is a worldwide business networking organization with over 7,000 chapters in over fifty countries. Misner has styled himself as something of a resident national expert on networking, and has written several books on the topic, all of which demonstrate the importance of networking and of course the excellence of his for-profit model. Naturally, as a long-lived organization with so many chapters and so many people, it obviously 'works', and given its size and scope, has no effective competitors.

This last fact is of particular interest, since the barriers to entry for a 'for profit' social VAR seem non-existent. Unlike global social networks like LinkedIn or Facebook whose scale provides a natural barrier to the entry of successful competitors, BNI chapters are self-sufficient, and provide business referrals from within the local chapter and not from other chapters regionally or nationally. Secondly, there is no financial barrier to entry, as each chapter meets in a common place, and unlike our farmer's market example, does not require dedicated physical infrastructure. The one barrier to entry that BNI has is an ability to advertise its presence through its members and through an on line institutional presence or 'brand'. This predefines to the masses what a social VAR should be and how it should be run. The problem is, it defines it incorrectly.

In the BNI interpretation, the social VAR consists of many individuals, not few. Indeed, BNI groups general number from fifteen to forty members. Secondly, the prerequisite is that members must have *different* professional interests, and not necessarily *complementary* professional interests. For example, a group may have an insurance adjuster, auto repair shop, telephony company, and IT consultant in the group, yet only the first two and last two have complementary professional interests. This means that different members will naturally form different circles of interest within the group within which they will mutually share referrals. Because BNI chapters contain different subgroups that within them have complementary interests, it may be described as an institution that has within each chapter several distinctive networking subgroups that only within them share common professional interests. In other words, BNI chapters represent conglomerates of private networks.

As a for profit social VAR, BNI certainly seems to meet our criteria for a successful business network. Within each chapter are individuals who have complementary professional interests, meetings are regular and cannot be skipped, and a token economy is in place to record who gave what referral to whom and to provide social pressure for members to provide referrals. Finally, the chapters are managed by a committee of individuals who handle everything from membership to training to finances. What it does uniquely have is a profit motive, but this comes at a price. This price is the unexpected cost of mixing individuals with complementary professional interests with those that have different professional interests. In other words, this pecuniary interest drives the economic success of BNI, but it comes at the cost of reducing sharply its value as a social VAR. It does this by neglecting the fact that professional interests and professional sales are often complex things that cannot be communicated in the large venue of twenty or so bobbling heads that comprise a BNI chapter meeting. If you have a product or service that requires more than two minutes (the BNI allotment per meeting) to get across, your group partners will not be able to properly explain your offerings to their clients, with the result that good referrals are never made, and poor referrals are more frequent.

The BNI program as set up works fine if all members have professions that are clearly and simply defined, but falls apart if individual members offer products and services that are not readily understood by the membership. The proof comes from the very members that BNI attracts. One of the distinguishing characteristics of BNI is that its membership derives from sales professions that market products and services that are easy to understand by virtue of our experience with them as individual consumers, or the so-called business to consumer model. As consumers, we understand complicated things like insurance, car repair, dentistry, and real estate sales because we *have* to know about them, and it is thus easy to refer such services and easy to inquire from a client about their present needs for them. However, business-to-business sales models represent products and services that are not subject to our individual experience as consumers, and salespeople in this model require a consultative approach to qualify clients and to make the sale. The result is that salespeople who sell products to other businesses are not well served by BNI since BNI meetings are not structured to facilitate a deep understanding of b-to-b products and the often-detailed qualifying questions necessary to secure a potential referral. B to b selling in other words does not cohere with the BNI way of referring, when the two-minute description of what you do in a BNI meeting is transformed into a member's ten second qualifying question to a potential referral who implicitly knows what you are talking about.

Even BNI has discovered how it's model does not apply to this mode of selling, as its b to b clone, called 'Corporate Connections' has faltered in public acceptance, and numbers but a tiny (11 chapters compared to the 7,000 chapters worldwide) fraction of chapters compared to its b to c cousin.

In sum, as a for profit social VAR, BNI brings knowledge and structure to networking, and even though member motivations are attributed to personal character or the 'givers gain' motto, BNI clearly adheres for the most part to the necessary structure of an effective barter economy for information. However, because BNI is a for profit organization, it also has the perverse incentive of growing the group beyond members who have complementary professional interests because a bigger group is simply more profitable, and if it adds members who can contribute only tangentially and drives out b to b salespeople, so be it. The problem is, BNI has not been frank with potential members that it is not as effective as a b to b networking group. This has been a recipe for criticism from former BNI members, who only from hard experience recognize the organization's limitations, and understandably recognize that they have been purposely oversold. Finally, as we will note in the next chapter, the BNI model can be easily replicated without the need to charge hundreds of dollars in fees and other expenses. The BNI secret it seems is no secret at all.

Given its benefits and limitations, does joining BNI bring value? It depends ultimately on the type of business you are engaging, but it also depends upon your level of understanding of how networks work as information economies. As we will see, this understanding demonstrates that BNI is not the wave of the networking future.

The information economies we have discussed indirectly add money to your pocket, but when the money happens to be play money for the participant, and real money for those who set up the information exchange, then we have networks that are immensely profitable for a select few yet are virtually empty for everyone else. These networks are called virtual networks, and as we will argue, are the networks you should dread.

Virtual Networks

Social Media: interactive communications media where people meet but never meet, have a million friends but no friends, make time but have no time, and have privacy and yet no privacy at all. Overall, social media represents a social regress called progress.

Social Network: *A way of easily developing anonymous business partners and best friends for life after you both met for fifteen seconds at a trade show and will never personally meet again. When coupled with a cold sore or brain infection, the social network is also known as a social disease.*

Token Economy: *Common in business social media, and involves the use of near worthless tokens to motivate business people. Thus, by giving them certificates, endorsements, likes, pokes and views, motivation is exponentially increased and everybody makes quota and then move on to better jobs and better tokens.*

To understand the original and most prolific virtual network, you need to just look in an obscure kitchen cabinet for a hefty yellow brick of a book that arrives at your doorstep once a year. The Yellow Pages is the original virtual network, although in the past it was soft bound and not software. As a social network however, the Yellow Pages fails, because outside of a common humanity shared by all those names and phone numbers, this is a network with a means of exchange inflated to worthlessness. Of course, you can puff up your credentials by buying a bigger yellow page ad, but marketing is *not* networking, and the Yellow Pages are not a forum to barter information. However, if you put a Yellow Pages of sorts on the internet, it can become a business network in name if not reality.

Given the mind-boggling number and geographic dispersion of your on-line business contacts (or, formerly your Yellow Pages business contacts), for the social network to succeed as a business network (as in a farmer's market) somehow the 'search' button must suffice. When the need strikes them, your business connections will somehow find you, like locating a certain DVD on Amazon, by just looking you up with the press of a key. As a primary exemplar of the virtual business network, LinkedIn trumps the other non-business networks such as Facebook by allowing you to sort your skills, interests, education, endorsements etc. into an online vitae that is exhaustively searchable. It is a boon to recruiters, who deal in the trade of the human product, namely you. For the rest of us however, its value is far less certain.

The question is whether that LinkedIn acquaintance of yours who needs a lawyer, plumber, or just a guy who can fix your electric wall socket (particularly if he is handy at all of these things) will look you up, or just go to the Yellow Pages (on line of course) or a personal reference or friend. If you look them up to do anything other than buy from them, you will be likely disappointed. Try getting something of value by 'inmailing' from LinkedIn somebody with a request for information, a referral, or some other information of value, and be prepared to do a lot of waiting. So, you wait for them to contact you, and wait. As you will doubtless discover, to expect more out of acquaintances because they list their social and business resumes is about as sensible as expecting them to follow up on you because of a business card swap and a hearty handshake. There is simply little or no incentive for them to do it, because at root the social network is *not* a business network at all. There is no store of information that can be traded, no means of tracking what is traded, and no commonly attended meeting place. In addition, there is no cost of entry into this network, no way to validate what is being claimed, and no way to determine the motivations of the folks who want to be on your network, or whether they are looking at you, your comments, or even looking out for your interests. Of course, LinkedIn is easily hyped as an effective business network because online business networks are an unfamiliar place full of easy promises.

Linked Out

In the amazingly stupid movie, 'The Jerk', our hero (Steve Martin) survived and prospered by doing amazingly stupid things. As an up and coming gas station attendant, one of his first great accomplishments was his new found entry in the phone book, which he held up to his boss as proof that he was an up and coming guy.

Of course, we don't hold up our listing in the phone book as proof of our rising status in the world, but we do have something that's much better, a personal listing, which we can also hold up to our boss and other significant others as proof that we are rising stars.

I certainly felt that way when I originally signed up for the business social network: LinkedIn. Having read the hype about the service and perused the LinkedIn 'how to' books at B. Dalton, which breathlessly described the service as the operating system for the business network, I was impressed. From the copious tricks, tips, and descriptions those books contained, it certainly seemed that effective networking was merely dependent upon how I list and advertise my presence. Like mastering that other operating system Windows 10, just apply yourself to understanding and using the user groups, endorsements, 'inmail', connections, discussion groups and what not, and you will be a business-networking dynamo in no time.

And so, I dutifully and with excitement entered my stuff, a resume of skills and accomplishment that reflected my sterling character and peerless capabilities. Of course, after this I had to let the world know, or at least the people I wanted to know. Unfortunately, by accident or design, I hit the wrong button, and 'recruited' everybody on my Yahoo mail account, all 500 plus of them, including folks who don't know me, or are like me, or are even 'like' me. It was a social embarrassment to be sure, and I was surprised that the ten or so folks who accepted the invitation to connect even remembered me, because I certainly couldn't remember them.

LinkedIn keeps you coming back for more because it is all about feedback about you and your colleagues. Unfortunately, the feedback happens to be the assorted career trivia that's of no consequence to you or your career. So, you get to know who is now newly connected to who, who changed a job, added a skill, got an endorsement, got a promotion, wrote a book (that's me of course, soon to be mentioned on my LinkedIn account), or just had a bad hair day. You also get to know how many people recently went to your profile, how many people you know, and how many people they know. It's all about the degrees of separation that demonstrate that we are only a connection or two from knowing everybody, just as tracing your family tree invariably links you to the family tree of George Washington or Christopher Columbus. Nonetheless, deep down you didn't want to know everybody, just as everybody doesn't want to know you.

But the feedback keeps coming, and even though it is near useless, we keep coming back for more. We want to know everybody who we don't want to know, and keep adding invitations to grow our score of contacts and recommendations and endorsements, even though their value is next to nothing. So, our reputation balloons out like a high-level mage in the on-line game Warcraft, yet your reputation is gamed because it is gamified. Indeed, LinkedIn has recently added an endorsement header to each profile, so you can endorse a selection of a colleague's skill sets that you otherwise have no earthly notion existed. But that's ok, since hopefully the individual whose leadership or cold calling skills you endorsed will return the favor by endorsing you. We have fun making all those endorsements, as if we will get credits in return. That's just the problem, for endorsements must be earned, and if they are given as freely as college credits from a diploma mill, our credentials become meaningless. For our personal and professional lives, reputation is everything, but reputation like money can be inflated and devalued if we replace it with a 'Monopoly' currency that can inflate your self-worth as you perceive yourself as an expensive property, except for the fact that owning Park Place and Boardwalk, for all its satisfactions, still does not pay the bills. However, in the penury that a reliance on LinkedIn guarantees, at least we have fun in our delusions.

Virtual networks are not networks because they do not meet the criteria of a barter information economy. Although members can sort themselves into more homogenous 'groups', this is no more different than segregating one's business in the yellow rather than white pages of a phone book. Just as a half page space in the Yellow Pages encourages a company to trump up its products and services, so too does the profile space on LinkedIn allow you to trump up your resume until you, like nearly all members, have the qualifications not only to run a Fortune 500 firm but the personal characteristics of a business renaissance genius and saint. LinkedIn ends up with a million chiefs and no Indians, as all its members become legends in their own minds.

LinkedIn ultimately fails as a business network because it articulates no rules *for* networking. You join the LinkedIn network, and follow up with adding your name in LinkedIn to an interest group, user group, or maybe a group of professionals who all went to Harvard, Yale, or Baskin Robbins. So what? It all doesn't matter unless you have rules that benefit all and that all must abide. No rules, no play, and that is true for a game of cards or the game of networking. You must have skin in the game to play the game. It requires effort as well as warranty, something LinkedIn does not have. But LinkedIn is right about one thing, private business networking to be truly successful on a global scale requires the web. All that is needed are commonly agreed rules of the game.

The Rules of the Game

If you were looking to find partners to play bridge, a pickup game of basketball, or just a marriage partner, with the internet you can now advertise for suitable partners, or better, find them on social sites that allow you to match your preferences, attributes, and skills with other people to find the perfect match. On line databases that advertise social networking can do these things because they assume that the involved parties know and will play by the rules that are established in the groups published bylaws, or are evident from commonly shared experience (e.g. dating sites). The rules are what you must know in advance when you arrive at the bridge game, basketball court, or even on a date. If the rules of how to play bridge, basketball, or behave on a date are unclear among the parties involved, these arrangements and the sites that mediate them can never, ever, work.

The overarching premise of this book is that the rules for business private networking are unclear, unworkable, and need to be replaced by simple and effective standards and procedures that are based on empirically or experienced based best practices. However, to the average businessperson, what are they? Is it a single lunch with a contact and the exchange of business cards, or is it the nucleus of a lead sharing network such as the business networks we described? Is it one meeting or several, are they frequent or infrequent, etc. Unlike acquaintance, vendor, professional, and for profit private networks (e.g. BNI), the absence of clear rules of engagement is a barrier to entry for any enterprising sort who wants to advertise for folks to join and participate in a private network. With networking groups like the Rotary, Chamber, or PTA, the rules are simple, easy to discover, and are thus easy to advertise. This is not so with private business networks.

Ultimately, the barrier to entry of a private business network is that there are no standardized social rules for private networks as compared to the social rules for all other networks from professional to private social networks (e.g., dating sites). Establishing a clear set of rules privately is but one-step away from establishing them publicly. It is only with publicly established standards can such an on-line presence be established.

The failure of virtual networking to replace business networking, and the fact that private networking to be successful refocuses our analysis on how to construct a business network in the real world of face-to-face meetings, contractual obligations, and truly shared value must change the rules of networking. How I propose we can do that follows next.

Chapter 3

The Rules of Networking

How to Network

In general, folks on the go don't want to learn why, they want to learn how. The why of course is important as a means of validating that what you are doing is the correct way, and to properly assign blame if you fail. In the popular literature on business, the how of recommended procedure and helpful hints is normally prefaced by a lengthy exhortation of why you should believe them that invariably revolves around you taking a leap of faith that the author actually knows what he is talking about. He proves his wisdom by the hearsay of examples of his own grand success that you would be wise to believe because you can't disprove them otherwise. Personal endorsements are not proofs, although we accept them as such, and I will not produce them here. Instead, the explanations offered in the first two chapters and the chapters to follow this one must suffice. The proof of my effort however is nudging you to provide the proof yourself through changing the way you network. Thankfully, that can be done in short order. (And yup, I can take the blame too if it doesn't work.) To do that one must shake the conviction that networking is hard that keeps you from networking in the first place. It's not.

Networking is hard when it has no explicit rules

Work can be hard because it requires a lot of physical or mental exertion. Physical exertion occurs when our muscles are strained, but mental exertion occurs when our patience is strained (although as we will later see, strained patience also strains your muscles). When your thinking is actually going somewhere, mental activity is actually a quite pleasurable and rewarding activity, but when it goes nowhere or is confused we become nervous and frustrated. Networking above all is a mental activity that unfortunately can try anyone's patience because we don't know the rules. Consider how frustrating and difficult a football game would be if the rules in advance were only partially known, or were interpreted differently by each player. Similarly, for networking, it just seems hard because the rules for networking are not clear, and not just for us, but for everybody else.

It is the lack of clarity that makes networking hard, for when we don't know what is expected from us in a networking environment from introductions to conversations to mutual demands, the lack of rules causes frustration and anxiety. Moreover, even if you do understand the rules of networking, if nobody else understands them, it doesn't help you much that you do. This is because your peers are not going to go along with your more insightful way of sharing business information.

For any economy to work, the rules must be understood and accepted by all participants. To understand how to network requires understanding how networks work and the specific rules by which they work. As a barter network of information, the rules of a business network are poorly understood, and even if explained must be successfully put to the test. You need explanation if you want to justify your behavior, but to just get started and take them for a test drive, just follow the simple rules below.

Rhyme and Reasons

There are two reasons to business network:

1) To meet someone who needs your product or service.

2) To meet someone who can market your product or service.

If you meet someone who may need your services, you can quickly guage that interest and arrange a second meeting on the spot. That translates a 'cold call' (an introduction and cordial conversation) into a sales call. However, a sales call represents a prospective transaction of money for services, and is not business networking because it does not represent the sole trade of non-monetary information. A trade of information is also not in the cards if you recruit someone you meet in a business social to resell your product or accept a retainer if they refer a client to you. A prospective trade of information *does* occur if you meet someone who has the means to refer you to many prospective clients in return for the prospect and incentive of receiving similar information. So where do you meet such people: a professional network.

Join a Professional Network

Join your local Chamber of Commerce or some similar professional network. The Chamber is by far the best bet because of its ubiquity, sizable membership, and strength and variety of its programs, ranging from community involvement to network socializing. In addition, its non-profit orientation ensures that upon joining you will not be sold snake oil (although you will invariably meet folks who will want to sell you scented candles and retirement plans).

Whatever professional network you do choose, go to their network socials, lunches, seminars, or any occasion where you can meet other folks who are gatekeepers for multiple customers, have a strong interest in networking (obvious because they are in a networking group), and have strong complementary professional interests with you and any other members of your own group. Of course, you will meet people who will want to buy your stuff now or in the future, but your real reason is to recruit them to your private network. The Chamber, like all other professional networks, is a primary place to effectively network because it is one of the best places to recruit people *to a* private network where real deal making occurs. But when you recruit them to your private network, how do you keep them there?

Essentials for a Private Network

Strong Complementary Professional Interest and Resources

A strong complementary professional interest is the primary requirement of an effective business network, augmented by having information to trade. If a participant has no clients or sees few prospective clients, he is not in a position to trade information with another professional who has many customers and prospects.

Know each other's products

Having a complementary interest is good enough if you are selling apples, pumpkins and grapes. If the ability to sell any of these was greatly enhanced with detailed knowledge about recipes, health benefits, and other advantages, your sales production would thus *require* that you sit with your partners and learn the features and benefits of their wares. This 'one-on-one' meeting is a requirement for for-profit social vars like BNI, and for good reason. The ability to be a productive member of a private network requires that you know in depth what each member sells, his preferred clientele, how on your part your clients may benefit from them, what clients you can refer to him, and vice versa. Indeed, without this, a member is participating blindly, subject merely to the hope that his colleagues will be looking out to their interests. Every new member should be encouraged if not required to have a one on one meeting from time to time (depending upon the quality of the information each can share with one another) with each fellow member, which will produce complementary knowledge, and help bind each member to the interests of the group.

Keep the Group Small

Two to ten regularly attending members are all you need for complex sales. For simple sales (advertising promos, real estate sales), the group can be much larger. Because high-end sales professionals (business to business) have complex products to sell, they need time to explain them to their network peers, as compared to low-end sales to professionals (business to consumer) whose products are simple and are commonly understood.

Meet Often

Multiple individual business affiliates require multiple meetings to stay in touch and trade information and leads. If you have for example five members in your group, it is difficult if not impossible to set up five separate meetings for one week let alone for succeeding weeks. It is best to meet them in one place that is conveniently accessible and have meetings that are short and to the point. Attendance does not have to be obligatory, but it does have to be often. Meetings should be scheduled every two weeks to start. If an affiliate cannot meet often enough, then find another.

Use a Token Economy

Have one incentive and memory suffices, have many of them that you give and receive and you need to know where they are, where they are coming from, and where they went. You in other words need to account for the debits and credits. We do that at work with spreadsheets, call reports, and CRM programs, and networks are no different. So, you count who refers what to who and when, and perhaps other information such as the result of the referral, joint calls, and other useful information.

Token economies, like all economies, must have a balance of payments, and if you have information worth 1000 tokens and your colleague has information worth 10, there is not much to exchange. Having Germany and Greece as a trading partners is not a good idea if both are on an equal footing.

With a token economy, you can 'monetize' your prospective, current, and legacy clients. Prospective clients are new customers you meet to sell, current clients are customers that you are selling to, and legacy clients are clients you have sold to. You may have only a need to visit the first of these, but your partner may have a need to see all of them. Thus if you have a client base of two hundred clients who you can meet but want nothing from you, you can still monetize them by trading joint calls with them with joint calls with your partners legacy clients.

Group Procedure

The nitty gritty of running a group should follow the KISS principle, or 'Keep It Simple, Stupid'. After all, you want to grow your business, not be a scoutmaster. The only merit badge that counts is creating new business. Besides, if the folks in your network are on the same page, they will appreciate your need to get to the point of why they are there.

Notification: Put together an email list that you can send weekly updates for the group, including reports, meeting dates, and other information of value, such as other social events where you can meet other professionals, and be introduced to them by fellow members.

Attendance: To accommodate the busy schedules of your members, but still provide maximum value, meetings should be bi-weekly to start. However, attendance must be reliable, and absences that are not due to pressing business, personal or other members should be infrequent. If they happen too frequently, cut the individual from the group and find a replacement.

Venue and Time: The venue for group meeting must be easy to get to, the meetings must occur at a convenient time, and must be relatively short, one-hour to ninety minutes' tops. The meeting should begin at a precise time and end at a precise time.

Reporting: Weekly reports (see sample in appendix) communicate what have you done for me lately? They are a ledger of the mutual exchanges of members, and score the relative contributions of members, not to mention provide an incentive for future contributions.

Discussion: If there is a new visitor to the group, have everyone in the group introduce themselves, their company, their company's major service or product, and ideal client. Then cut to the chase. Do a round robin with all attendees and discuss:

a) Clients you have seen and the ones will you see.

b) What you have and will talk about and how you have expanded the customer conversation to include the interests of group members

c) Clients both active and inactive you *have* or *will* personally introduce a group member to in the coming week either separately or jointly. (A personal introduction or a joint call is *not* necessarily a sales call, but because a salesperson (and doubtless, her sales manager as well) gauges her success by the fullness of her appointment calendar, and because she is far more adept at quickly qualifying a lead than you will ever be, scheduling joint calls will likely be the primary measure of the group's success.)

d) Specific companies you would like to meet.

e) One on one meetings you have had with other members.

Once this is completed, set aside a few minutes for your members to discuss their products and services, their ideal client, projects they are working on presently, and their future prospects. If time permits, put the spotlight one member so they can expound on these issues in more detail. Finally, a ledger summary of who is working with who and with what prospects will be given to all members.

Management: Simplicity is key. One person should run the group, with a second member available for backup in case you are unavailable. There is no need for membership, education, finance or other committees. No dues should be charged until management adds additional value (e.g. web site, event hosting, etc.).

Divide and Conquering

The biggest advantage and disadvantage of a b-to-b network is that it may grow. This isn't much of a problem if membership fees are your object, and indeed it is a source of profit for b to c networks such as BNI that puts a premium of profit above group effectiveness. As networks grow, they can become balkanized, with subgroups in the network (say, finance types like bankers, brokers, and insurance agents) referring more clients between themselves than to other members. In addition, b-to-b networking requires that each member lend an attentive ear to the offerings of his peers. Grow the group too large and you end up a group of bobble heads who only have a marginal amount of time to discuss their interests, and interpersonal bonds become more difficult to grow and sustain.

The answer to this problem is to simply divide the group into two groups that have more complementary interests. Thus, you may break a group of twelve into two subgroups of six that separately have much more in common. From there, you can build up each group as before, allow intergroup referrals and even combined group meetings or other social events from time to time. As each group grows, they can again be divided amoebae like, until you have multiple b-to-b groups to manage. So, what's in it for the entrepreneurial type who wants to manage more than one b to b group? If he is the sole representative of a career field (e.g. telephony), his telephone referrals should increase since he is the only referral partner for his field across all groups. He is 'paid' for his effort by not

having to share referrals with another telephony salesperson who may be in
another group.

Problems

A private network (or social VAR if adhering to formal rules) is simple in concept, difficult in execution, and uncertain in prospect. Thus, you want to start out slow, act conservatively, constantly experiment, and explain everything you do.

Start with Two: Start small with a network of two. Get comfortable with the rules of your network, your mutual dedication to it, and its immediate and future promise, and then invite others to join who have complementary interests. When you invite new members to attend, whet their appetite to keep attending by giving them something for the pleasure of their company, such as a promise of a joint call, referral, or other benefit to be received within a few days. Also, keep meeting times regular, but not too often or too infrequent. A meeting every two weeks is likely to be in the 'Goldilocks' zone for all parties involved.

Get to and keep on point

Follow the script of the meeting and resist the temptation to chat on other things. Like nearly all business meetings, network meetings also tend to be major time wasters. It's nice to be in a group, to have chummy conversations, and with mutual assent, to get totally off track until the hour beckons and you must spend at least a minute or two on matters at hand. A warm feeling after the meeting does not signify a good meeting, the firm prospect of future appointments and referrals does. If the meeting does not end up with these, it has failed.

Explain, Explain, and Explain some more…in writing

If you invite new people to your network, you do not want to spend your time continually justifying the rules of the group and why it should succeed. Give them a manual, not a lecture. The psychology of networking is not a simple thing, nor is it written in stone. This book offers a starting template, and hopefully a good enough explanation to start, and the best explanations are never final. So give them this stuff to read, and reserve your network meetings for networking, not explanations of networking.

Don't expect it to be easy.

Private networks are uncommon. Sales people do not use them like they could, treating them too often as mere avenues to socialize. Trading referrals takes some getting used to, and many folks don't want to get used to it. So expect the novelty and not the logic of our proposition to work against you. You will experience initial turnover, so keep recruiting new potential members.

Dealing with Inadequate Professional Networks

Professional networks succeed as networking groups because of the private networks they engender. However, because the managers of professional networks do not know how a private network 'works', the professional network becomes far less useful. Like awkward teens at a school dance who know how to dance but not how to date, socializing skills do not translate into networking skills. *Networking skills must be learned.* Indeed, networking skills are very different from social skills, and a major reason why professional networks churn through members is that they do not impart networking skills to new members or help them advertise or promote the existence of private networks founded from the group to other members. It thus becomes more difficult to meet those individuals that you would need to meet, or find like-minded private networks that you can join. They are in the membership roster of course, but not at the meetings. The fact that professional networks may not be the optimal place to meet like-minded professionals speaks to the limitations of how professional networks are run.

Nonetheless, there are work arounds. For the Chamber of Commerce for example, participation in the executive level of the chamber or as new member ambassadors present one with the opportunity to meet members who would not otherwise appear at Chamber social functions. As we shall see, it doesn't have to be that way.

The Network of Networks

The networking group par excellence is one of the oldest, and although it as an institution it is an 'institution'. Chambers of Commerce are a local group of businesses whose goal is to advance mutual business interests both among each other and as an advocate of business interests to the public and to political institutions. Membership can be a matter of civic obligation, in which case an organization joins but scarcely participates, or it can involve the active participation of businesses to lobby, network, and advertise among each other.

Like membership in the Better Business Bureau, Chamber membership is a badge of civic responsibility, not a predictor of civic participation. Indeed, from the expansive directory of members that are a Chamber's pride, the vast majority do not participate in Chamber functions at the level they could. But why?

The simplest reason may be one of competition. Other networking groups from the Rotary to the local PTA duplicate the lobbying, civic, and socializing programs offered by the Chamber. A second reason may be the assumption that people of diverse professions and interest may want to meet up because of that diversity alone. However, it is argued that business people of different professions are brought together by the primary interest they share, not by the individual interests they occasionally share. Thus, a group of diverse professionals may get together to hear the Mayor speak at a chamber event, but not because they may have the off chance of sitting next to someone who can educate them on how wireless networks work or even sell him one. Indeed, invite a group of diverse professionals to a meeting that has no unifying purpose except the pleasure of each other's company, and few if any will likely show up.

What other networking groups do not offer represents the Chamber's greatest and most understated strength, its focus on growing local businesses, which of course means sales. The Chamber is an effective interest and social network, but its unique effectiveness as a business network lies in its importance as a promoter of new and established businesses, and as a social intermediary for private networks that drive sales. The Chamber in other words promotes business growth, and through its social functions mediates the growth of private networks. The problem, as is common with all professional networks, is that it doesn't recognize the importance of private networks, and therefore does not facilitate the growth and understanding of private networks as a matter of policy that ultimately entails educating its members in the psychology of networking. The result is that membership and chamber participation trend lower because members just don't know how to network. The care and feeding of private networks is left to the devices of the individual member (uninformed and haphazard) and the for profit private network (BNI) (informed and hazardous) who will set them up and advertise them for you. But whereas for profit networks are diminished by the perverse incentive of revenue growth that compromises effective business networking, the chamber as a nonprofit is diminished because it focuses on the incentives of civic responsibility, education, and other member services that overshadow a proper consideration of the incentives for greater participation in business networking that focuses on sales.

The Chamber could do the latter by doing two things: 1) educating its new and present members on the psychology and practice of networking, and 2) listing the private networks founded by members so other members can find them. If that strategy sounds familiar, it should. Ivan Misner, the founder of BNI, wrote several books on networking to educate the masses (my book reviews on his stuff at the end of this book). He stressed education in networking for BNI members, listed BNI chapters on the web so people could easily find and contact them, and unsurprisingly argued that good networking ends if it doesn't already begin with for profit private networks like BNI. Since there is only one networking group of BNI's stature and scope, it figures that other networking groups must be measured against the standard of the preeminent private network, which in his case is BNI. The major irony that Misner does not address is that if professional networks like the Chamber linked their purpose with the care and feeding of private networks, BNI would soon be out of business, and that the Chamber would be a magnet for all businesses. Maybe in the future it will.

Dealing with Inadequate Co-Marketing

Are your networking partners promoting your wares with the same skill and acumen that you do? Almost certainly they are not. After all, it takes a professional salesperson months of training and practice to be able to quickly interest and qualify a client, and you certainly have much more of an incentive than your networking partner. You are left with the promise that they will look out for your interest, a promise that usually goes rarely or partially fulfilled. The solution to this is to take matters into your own hands, and simply go along with your colleague on a joint call.

A joint call is not a joint presentation, but merely involves you tagging along with your colleague when he makes his sales rounds. Given whatever rationale your partner chooses (learning the ropes, just visiting, in for the weekend), invariably his customer will ask you what you do for a living, and you will have your three minutes of fame to involve, qualify, and perhaps secure his permission for a future appointment. For a sales professional, three minutes is often all that's necessary.

One of the advantages of a joint call is that its prospect makes your attendance and participation in the group more valuable. Simply being told that an effort is being made on your behalf is hardly as effective as being on the front row when that effort is being made, or better, making that effort yourself. Its importance as an incentive is similarly accentuated if joint calls are listed in the weekly activity report to your group members.

The Joint Call

One of the ironies of a web connected world is that as we become less personally connected being virtually connected is a suitable replacement. The success of relationships matters when it is metered. Thus, you are a more successful fellow if you have 5000 connections, 20000 friends, and 100000 who read your tweets. Your relationships are a mile wide, but a millimeter deep, and shallowness somehow translates into personal and business success.

An effective business network requires that your partners actively look out for your interest. Nevertheless, regardless of their interest, effort, and enthusiasm, they are a poor substitute for you. After all, they possess little of the training, motivation, and presence that you can bring to bear to gain the attention of your wares. A good salesperson can qualify an account within minutes and given the right 'elevator pitch', gain permission to carry on with a client for another day. So why not bring your partner with you for those three precious minutes that he can take in front of your client before he recedes dutifully in the background? Why bother with the uncertainty of securing a lead when you can certainly make an introduction?

The prospect of arranging a joint call rather than a lead cuts to the core of every salesperson's daily agenda and personal motivation, namely meeting with new prospective clients who will give them at least a minute of their time. A joint call is easy to arrange (and a cinch to arrange if you toss in lunch for the client as well), it generally does not require a client's permission (although it is helpful to ask), and gives a salesperson a quick audience rather than a deferred and uncertain lead. It makes the results of a network partnership immediate and tangible. In addition, it makes visits to legacy clients who have marginal value for a sales call into tradable assets, as a partner may introduce you to her own legacy client in return. A joint call is built upon the prospect and not certainty of a sales presentation. Because the client is not expecting a presentation, the joint caller will speak when spoken to, and invariably, she is.

The proof of concept of a joint call occurs when the salesperson you are calling with just happens to be you. This happens when a client knows that you represent a separate persona and/or professional interest that are to his interest. For example, a male cheerleader couples his professional interest in cheerleading with his personal interest in meeting girls. Similarly, the personal interests of a volunteer 'ambassador' for the Chamber of Commerce who visits with new members is not long hidden, as your true interest 'comes out' when you engage in conversations, as if the real you pops out from disguise. Thus if you are meeting lots of folks in a church, social or other informal group, when the conversation segues to 'what do you do for a living?', this is the time for you to briefly remark upon your unique trade (lawn mowing, insurance sales, etc.). This will hopefully secure their interest and perhaps a meeting to discuss it in the future.

In this manner, each member also gains an understanding of her colleagues' products and services in the context of a client call, has an opportunity to understand the client better, and suggest services that may be offered to them in the future.

The Making of a Social VAR

Becoming an expert in one's field and/or complementary fields that are represented by your network colleagues indirectly increases your sales through reciprocal referrals, and much more. It is simply the tried and true VAR strategy made 'social'. By being able to speak fluently across complementary sales fields (e.g., telephony, IT, and web design), you become more important to your client by being more capable of providing integrated and not piecemeal solutions, and that will translate into greater customer loyalty and increased sales.

As a formalized private network, a Social VAR network *supplements* some networks (client), *complements* others(vendor networks), *replaces* or *modifies* still others (interest, private and for profit networks), and are *dependent* on still others (professional networks). Nonetheless, the sales professional may still undervalue a private network if it does not cohere with her sales style. If a salesperson believes that personal relationships, narrow technical knowledge, polished closing techniques or mere hard work (e.g. lots of cold calls, great customer service) are the key to sales success, then the private network becomes far less important. But if this is not true, and can be empirically demonstrated to be not true, then salesmanship becomes not a matter of individual but communal effort. That would entail a new way to think about sales that makes proper networking essential to sales success, and change dramatically the role of the salesperson. It is this new science of sales that we will address next.

Accounting for it All: Use a Simple and free CRM

As a final note, using information to build a successful network means you must account for it, and like an accountant you must know where it goes, where it is coming from, and when it is due. A customer relationship management system is necessary to keep it in place. It must be simple, powerful, and free. This author recommends the Capsule CRM system as the best of the lot, and the price of 0$ fills the bill. https://capsulecrm.com/

Chapter 4

The Ends of Sales

From Barter to Sales: A return to the farmer's market

When we last left Bob, Tom, and Danielle, they were running an efficient and profitable barter network that kept them fully in stock with pumpkins, grapes, and apples. What need is there for money in this picture, or for any of these individuals to sell their product to each other? In short, it is when there is a matter of unequal demand. The three can go on trading their products with one another as long as the debits and credits eventually even out or nearly even out. However, if Bob and Tom begin to sell lots and lots of apples, then the books of the token economy will be thrown out of whack, and Danielle, who has far less need of pumpkins and grapes, has to find another means of compensation. Danielle in other words needs to get paid.

Human life is a continual give and take, and we can generally get by through bartering a please or thank you in exchange for someone holding open the door for you or performing any small favor. Borrow the neighbor's lawnmower for five minutes, and a thank you will suffice. Borrow if for a week, and you should offer to mow his lawn in return. Borrow it each week, and you need to pay him for the favor. The content of payments moves from a barter exchange of platitudes to a monetary exchange of dollars for services when the imbalance of exchanges grows. Our social networks thus become sales networks when the trade imbalance becomes too great. When the information imbalance becomes too large, you have to charge for it, and the prospect of that imbalance and a possible fee provides the incentive to transform a barter exchange into a monetary sale as soon as possible.

The prospect of an information imbalance is much less if both parties have the same level of knowledge, as is demonstrated when groups of similar professionals band together in trade groups. Members of trade groups exchange information more freely knowing that they will gain more or less equally in the exchange, whereas this is not the case when the interests and knowledge of a group of professionals are dissimilar. For example, sit next to a lawyer and you can get only so much information before he sets you up for a paid consultation, but if you are a lawyer then you can talk for hours about case law knowing that the information you give will be returned in kind.

When significant information imbalances occur, you need to get paid to redress the balance. The act of presenting the case that there is an imbalance and that payment is necessary for setting it straight makes you into a salesperson. However, a monetary incentive not only balances your accounts, but incents you to move them out of whack again so you can ask for even more money to put them again in balance. So a doctor, lawyer, and car repairman are perversely incented not to resolve the balance, but to grow it. The patient ends up needing a few more tests, a project a few more billable hours, and an auto a few more repairs. You the client know and suffer from this, with the result that salespeople are not to be trusted or dealt with. Is the fact that salespeople cannot argue against their paychecks an inevitable outcome for the sales professional?

Death of a Salesman

Perverse Incentive: Known to afflict salespeople and everybody else earning a living, and cause them to follow their paycheck rather than their clients' true needs, resulting in a mis-fit between what is wanted and what is actually delivered. When the client invariably finds this out, it reduces the status of the salesperson to that of a misfit.

Salespeople are not popular or understood, outside and even within their profession. They are commonly viewed as an obnoxious, duplicitous, imposing, scheming, greedy, and even lazy bunch, and in the era of the internet are becoming wholly irrelevant. In fact, to be *marketed* to is a necessity of life, but to be *sold* to is an unnecessary and avoidable fact of life. That's the uncomfortable role of the contemporary salesperson. After all, people can just look up the facts on the internet, or follow the crowd to the source of truth. See a commercial on car insurance and we put up with a stupid green lizard, awful gags, and precious little content, but to listen to a car insurance salesperson who would actually tell you something of substance, you would rather enter the 9th circle of hell.

So, what is to distinguish the salesperson from a knowledgeable and trusted friend whose buying advice you will agree to in a minute? According to the social psychologist Douglas Kenrick, it's simple. *"In brief, we are inclined to go along with someone's suggestion if we think that person is a credible expert (**authority**), if we regard him or her as a trusted friend (**likeability**), if we feel we owe them one (**reciprocity**), or if doing so will be consistent with our beliefs or prior commitments (**consistency**). We are also inclined to make choices that we think are popular (**consensus**), and that will net us a scarce commodity (**scarcity**). We follow these general rules because they **usually** work to lead us to make the right choice. But because we often use them unthinkingly they are commonly exploited by compliance professionals* *and con artists, many of them wearing nice business suits, religious robes, or reassuringly friendly smiles."*

In other words, it's those evil exploitive salespeople up to no good again! Because of the very real danger of exploitation, as a salesperson you are not generally viewed at first as a credible expert *or* a trusted friend. Your prospective customer doesn't owe you anything, you don't want to be consistent with his beliefs (otherwise you can sell him nothing), and you certainly won't be popular with the unsold masses (who are happy with the status quo). You need to somehow reason from authority and demonstrate that you can get your clients a scarce new commodity, namely greater insight or knowledge, or a teaching moment. But first, you must earn his trust. Like a fearful deer in your headlights, you must get him to want to approach you.

One way that helps is good marketing. If you represent a brand that is trustworthy (Cadillac, IBM, Maytag, and even Geico), folks will be a bit more receptive to meeting with you to discuss their value. If you have no brand (Fisker Auto, Bob's Computers, Acme Appliances, or Lizard Insurance), expect to have a very lonely life in sales. On the other hand, if they think they know the value of your products already, even a good brand won't get you through the door. So as a computer reseller you may represent all the major brands, but not be able to get an appointment with a decision maker because the client believes they know all they need to know about the products and services you offer.

You of course disagree, which is why you are in sales to begin with. So how do you gain entry into the inner sanctum of your potential client? Cold calling won't help much unless you like talking to answering machines (which have spawned robo-cold callers in response), and are hopeful that you catch someone who somehow has recognized a need for your stuff and hasn't called you or a similar salesperson yet or bought the darn thing on Amazon.

Because you cannot trade on your authority or reputation, you need to trade on someone else's. So you rely upon a referral from a client, VAR, friend, or acquaintance that is given to you freely or upon your request. In other words, you rely upon your business networks to provide you referrals. Whether qualified or unqualified, simply mentioning the referring party increases your likelihood of making contact with your prospect, but even that's not enough if there is not proper incentive for your referral sources to give you the number of referrals you need. For a truly successful sales person, there are never enough referrals. You need your referral sources to work harder for you. That executive buddy of yours at the credit union, construction company, or accounting firm has lots of contacts, but nonetheless needs to work a lot harder for you to help you fill out your appointment calendar. As we have argued earlier, they won't do this out of the goodness of their hearts, but only if the incentive is there for them to do so. If they owe you a favor due your good work, strong personal relationship, or other favors you have provided for them in the past, then you can ask them to go the extra mile for you to not just provide but qualify referrals to you. If not, you can forget it. Nonetheless, you still need something more, and that is where private networks come in that are sustained by the mutual exchange of referrals, and as we will note referrals are important in more ways than one.

Networks to the Front!

A referral is an introduction to a client, but it does much more to help facilitate the sale because it redeems the salesperson in the client's eyes. The referral is the salvation of the salesperson because it warrants trust *in* the salesperson. People know there are information imbalances, they are just wary of those who will overstate them or just make them up, and end up not fixing the imbalance and overcharging them to boot. They in short know that they need to be sold to, they just want the sale to be valid and fair, not to be harassed afterwards, and they want an implied warranty to that effect. Referrals are just that, a personal warranty that the referred party will be a fair dealer and when the pitch is done, leave the client alone. This is where the value of business networks come to the fore. Whereas companies can warrant the service or product, business networks can warrant the accuracy of the *presentation* of that service of product, and as we will see, even discover the imbalances that call for the presence of a salesperson. However, even given the power of a qualified referral, there are reasons why they do not have a greater role in the sales process.

The Halo Effect

Put up a billboard, set up a web site, or open a restaurant touting Acme Autos, Bob's Accounting Service, or Chuck's hamburgers, and no matter the excellence of your wares you are immediately handicapped by a lack of reputation. Nobody in short knows whether to trust you or not. It's easier of course to walk through a business door holding a business card with an IBM logo than a Brand X computer company because the former has an established brand that signifies that you mean what you say, and many other things that don't need to be said.

Branding is dependent not just upon the company you are, but also upon the company you keep. If you have a reputation of serving reputable customers, and having partners who are reputable, then your authority is extended by your business partners and associates, who will vouch for your professionalism, product, integrity and that you are not a sales lizard. Of course, it helps to tag along with them to get the full benefit of their personal aura, but regardless of how your business colleagues transfer their credibility to you, the fact remains that credibility is not an aspect of your brand, it is your brand. In addition, halo effects make cold calling palatable because if you are serving the customer next door, or a client your customer personally knows, it is easier to walk through a door or call a potential client. Halo effects represent indirect rather than direct referrals, because your creditability and trustworthiness is inferred from the company you keep. No matter the source, with credibility, you can blabber inanities like the Geico lizard all day and still end up getting the green.

Networks to the Rear!

Business networks are critical to arrange the sales introduction, but not necessarily for the sales presentation. If a client, acquaintance, friend, or colleague in a private network refers you to a potential customer, you acknowledge your referral source briefly as you begin your meeting, and then you never mention them again. You can reciprocate with a thank you to your clients, acquaintances, and friends, but rarely do you feel obliged to reciprocate in kind to your private network colleague by expanding your business conversation with your other clients to include their products and services. Unfortunately, a thank you to your business colleague is simply not enough to encourage him to continue to provide you with referrals. However, there is more than simple whim that explains your decision to ignore your private network or 'social vars'. You don't bring up your private network and discuss the offerings of your colleagues in that network for several reasons:

1) You won't get anything in return.

You refer your client to a member of your private network. But what's in it for you? You can't enforce reciprocation. Indeed, your partner may not be able to reciprocate, and in time the memory of your referral fades. You can't in other words monetize your good deed, save for the faint hope, often amplified by motivation and sales mavens, that givers eventually gain. Unfortunately, sales karma has about as much empirical verification as the spiritual kind. You may indeed go to sales heaven, but not in this world.

2) You don't know how to make a referral.

If your partner sells solutions that are already understood, then it's easy to make a referral. A brief question can qualify them for your partner in real estate, care, repair, or insurance sales. However, if your partner sells solutions that are readily *mis*understood, then you are likely just as ignorant about them as your clients, and are far less capable of making a properly qualified referral. You need knowledge that you don't have the time or inclination to get, and unless you see some return on that investment, namely a complementary referral, you are most unlikely to make it.

3) You don't need to make a referral.

You get enough referrals from your company's marketing efforts and from clients, vars, or social networks that are reciprocated by good service, direct sales, or simple friendship, not by complementary referrals from your private network. If you don't cultivate your private network, it scarcely impacts your sales success. Furthermore, you sell because of excellent customer support, the hard drudge of cold calls, or the ability to recite the features and benefits of your products to appreciative clients. Expanding your sales conversation to include the products and services of your private network is unnecessary and at best superfluous to your sales success. So your private network becomes weak or perhaps non-existent.

The Customer Conversation

Ultimately, the importance of a business network depends upon whether you believe that all your customer needs is for you to recite the features and benefits of the products and services that your company offers and how they fit needs or remedy problems. If this is the case, there is no requirement to bring in the products and services of the members of your private network because the conversation does not need to be expanded beyond the problem solving issue at hand. There is in other words no need to bring in other business partners if your sales focus is narrow.

For example, an insurance agent can provide many types of insurance policies, an investment advisor many types of investment instruments, and an IT company many types of computing solutions. For sales success, their product line is all they will cover in a sales call. In these cases you are there to focus on a narrow aspect of his business that is served by the products and services you offer. The latter approach is called *features and benefits* sales. You recite how product attributes can fix the problem at hand, and you get the sale. This type of salesmanship is simple. The customer tells you the problem, and you offer the solution.

However, if you are interested in how he runs his business and how he can run it better, then you are likely to have the incentive to ask questions that extend beyond your product offerings and include the products and services of your professional colleagues. You do not give him mere solutions; rather, you teach him new perspectives that provide a new way to *integrate* solutions. Whether your partners in your private network reciprocate by expanding their conversation to include *your* wares is secondary to your role as a general advisor, not just a problem solver. You bring your private network partners in regardless of their interest in providing reciprocal referrals to you. A general advisor couches his solutions within the context of understanding how they integrate within the broader interests of the enterprise. An IT solutions provider for example will show how his solution may be integrated with telephony, web design, logistics, operations, and even how the enterprise will finance it all. As a salesperson, you in turn will explain how your solution integrates with other aspects of his business or other product needs to provide a comprehensive solution, and as a matter of course bring in your business partners through qualified referrals. The solution therefore rises beyond a mere recitation of facts to an explanation of how the enterprise works, and how your solution can help the organization work a lot better.

In contrast to a features and benefits sales approach, an *explanatory* sales style provides a solution that fits into the context of a thriving organization whose needs are interwoven, and that never stand alone. In other words, solutions are not sold merely because of what they do, but also how they work in the context of the overall needs of the business enterprise. You want to deeply understand the organization, and therefore you can provide solutions that narrower sales approaches can never do. It makes you more valuable to that organization, not as a narrow solutions provider, but as a teacher of new insights that through the implementation of yours and others products and services show how an organization can work better.

This explanatory sales style *challenges* clients because it goes beyond a descriptive features and benefits style that merely adheres to the customer's needs. Because your explanation is invariably different or at odds with his own, you are in effect challenging him to change his enterprise for the better through adopting your advice. Well and good, but is this prescription correct? Does challenging a client through an explanatory sales style work? As we will see, the data that decide the matter are unequivocal and surprising. But first, we must take the measure of what we don't know about sales and the principles behind sales success. As it is, we know a lot less than we think.

The Wayward Sales Model

Sales models have a way of avoiding challenge, refutation, or proof. If you heed the advice of a sales guru, trainer, or speaker, and fail, it's not because their approach hardly works, but that you didn't work hard. Sales models are hard to disprove because they depend upon aspects of intrinsic (and thus hidden) motivation that only the salesperson can provide. Secondly, they are dependent upon the nuance of procedure that can accept little deviation. Success depends upon the pithy questions, answers, statements, and closing questions that are as finely honed as a well-prepared resume or elevator pitch. It's a three minute drill with the creativity going into the polishing and practicing, not the thinking. Sales is at once eminently inscrutable (you ultimately supply the motivation and the wits) and predictable (know how to pitch and close). This is all fine as it goes, except it ignores one major factor: why the customer would want to listen to you in the first place, and *keep* listening to you. What is it that makes the customer feel that meeting you is the right and reasonable thing to do, and after the meeting considers that it was the right and reasonable thing to do, regardless of whether a sale was made?

The short answer is that we don't know, and there is no universally accepted principle for sales success. And what is its proof? It comes through a simple analysis of a uniformly held and uniformly misunderstood principle that makes true salesmanship the province of a select few that odds are does not include you.

Pareto's Principle

Pareto Principle: *An immutable economic law that proves that sales people are slouches, since only 20% are doing 80% of the work, when compared to other dynamic economies where 53% of the people are doing the work (US Economy) or 99% of the people doing the work (Chinese Economy).*

Consider a bizarre day at the office. You are a new accountant, and on your first day at the office, your supervisor hands you a brand new abacus. While you fiddle the little marbles around on the rails, you notice some of your peers have calculators, others use pc spreadsheets, and still others use sophisticated software to help them do work that is equivalent to yours. You are further confused by the job requirements. Some accountants have taken only a few college courses in accounting, others many, and still others have CPA certificates. Naturally, with such a hodgepodge of tools and capabilities, it will come as no surprise that a select few (the CPA's with computers) will far outpace the novices with ancient Chinese adding machines. The irony is that if all the accountants used the same tools, and adhered to the same standards of professional knowledge, quality performance would not skew to some fortunate few. Excellence in accounting depends upon using best tools, best procedures, and best education. Since these are universally held and adhered to, you can expect 100% of accountants in an accounting firm to do 100% of the work. There is in other words very little variance in the performance because performance is wholly predictable.

Now consider a normal day at the sales office, which being sales, is bizarre enough. You are new salesperson, and on your first day at the office you are handed a list of phone numbers to begin cold calling. While you fruitlessly dial for dollars, you notice that some of your colleagues are getting leads from VARs, others from established clients, and still others from colleagues in their private network or the marketing department. You are further confused by the different sales styles of your peers. Some focus on customer service, others focus on relationship building, and still others on educating their clients on the features and benefits of the company's products. You recognize that you are not on a level playing field, but rather a sales mine field, and as your results get blown away by your peers you get the keys to the 80% club, you slacker!

Excellence in sales depends upon best procedures to access leads and best procedures to sell to those leads. Often these two are separated, so that leads are acquired by good marketing, and sales are closed by good sales practices. If you are fortunate to have qualified leads handed to you through good advertising, sales can be easy, and even just a matter of order taking that often requires clerks, not salespeople. However, if you were hired to sell, invariably you will have to secure your own leads. If you are entering an established sales organization, expect that your peers will have their own source of leads and sales styles that leave you in their wake. Because the supply of what a salesperson works on (leads) and how they work on it (sales style) is so uncertainly determined, expect that sales success will be skewed to those fortunate few who have the means and capability to succeed that is not shared with those eighty percent or so who are not so endowed by happenstance or training.

Needless to say, this misdistribution of sales assets (leads) and sales style can be a cause of great stress within the organization.

If a firm hires folks of equal talent, equal performance cannot skew because of unequal capabilities, but because of unequal advantages in tools and clients. The lie to the Pareto Principle is that it is too often used to disparage the personal rather than situational aspects that cause performance to gravitate to a select few. Wrongly, it is used to support the assumption that salesmanship cannot be taught or is difficult to teach, and that individual differences rather than situational differences are the cause of wide variances in performance between the 'stars' and the also ran's. Because new salespeople in particular sense this bias in sales management, envy and dissatisfaction in a company can rise due to a misdistribution of sales 'wealth' that is not due to different skills, but different opportunities. Since 80% are not doing their job, then it is ok to disrespect, devalue, and displace that part of your sales force. If you are a member of the 80%, it is hard to be a member of any discipline when ineffectiveness is assumed to be so rooted in the salesperson herself. Although it is granted that individual sales people will always possess differences in temperament, education, and intelligence, such is the case for individuals of any profession. If sales people are carefully selected, the regression in their progress to an unsatisfactory mean with only a few sales outliers (the lucky 20%) must be attributed to other factors that can and should be addressed by management. This requires sales management to not only look at the different sales styles of its salespeople, but the different business networks that they use to succeed.

One reason that sales management does not look into this is because it does not know what to look for. Up to now there has not been any satisfactory proof that one sales or lead generation style is preferable to another. Thus, it should be expected also that your organization will have no unifying sales principle that will address the art of getting leads and the art of making the sale simply because one does not exist. If anything, this uncertainty will sway the organization from one sales fad to another, while all the while the Pareto Principle stands firm.

Because sales is so critical to the enterprise, and because the sales literature in general neglects rigorous proof, sales is regarded more as an art form rather than a science. Because it is not a science, the literature on sales attracts a crowd of hustlers, scoundrels, true believers, academics, pundits, and evangelists who may or may not know sales, but are certainly good at salesmanship. What they have not done is run the data to conclusively prove that they've got the goods on how to sell. If the data are called to speak, they as we shall see will leave only one contender standing.

The Challenger Sale

"…what sets the best suppliers apart is not the quality of their products, but the value of their insight-new ideas to help customers either make money or save money in ways they didn't even know were possible." Matthew Dixon and Brent Adamson [53]

As we have argued, business networking helps immeasurably to get the customer appointment, since a qualified referral from a peer your client trusts gives you the credibility to gain an audience with the customer. But once in front of the customer whose needs are clear, does a highly scripted and predictable sales pitch work? The key word in this question is 'predictable', because in times past when specialized knowledge was expensive or burdensome to come by, new knowledge could best be attained when it was hand delivered. The internet has of course changed all that, and you can expect that your customer is well versed and unsurprised by your wares. Why do you need to bring a brochure, handout, or white paper on your product to a meeting when your client can find them all with the click of a mouse? Because the customer has ready availability of product knowledge, the features and benefits model has lost much of its luster. With so much knowledge abounding about the nature and quality of products and services of almost any salesperson, why do you need a salesperson to begin with? How in other words has an age when information is instantly discoverable and free changed the way sales works?

This was the question posed by the Corporate Executive Board, a privately run sales 'think tank', which wanted to answer this question not theoretically, but by simply asking sales managers and salespeople, lots and lots of them, what was critical to sales success. To answer this question, it is helpful to discuss what types of salespeople there are. From their data derived from the interview of over six thousand sales reps and managers, the CEB derived five separate sales styles that reflect distinctive sales personalities that in most cases have their individual advocate in the popular sales literature. In this sales typology, each salesperson has a corresponding (although not exclusive) style, a corresponding philosophy, and a corresponding sales screed endorsed by one of those countless authors who show you how to do it.

The five types of sales people may be summarized into five categories: the hard worker, the relationship builder, the lone wolf, the reactive problem solver, and the challenger.

The Hard Worker *Hard workers are exactly who they sound like. They are the reps who show up early, stay late, and are always willing to put in the extra effort. They are the 'nose to the grindstone' sellers. They're self-motivated and don't give up easily. They'll make more calls than just about anyone else on the team. And they enthusiastically and frequently seek out feedback, always looking for opportunities to improve their game.*

The Relationship Builder *Just as the name implies, Relationship Builders are all about building strong personal and professional relationships and advocates across the customer organization. They're very generous with their time and work very hard to ensure that customer's needs are met. Their primary posture with customers is largely one of accessibility and service. "Whatever you need," they'll tell customers. "I'm here to make that happen. Just say the word."*

The Lone Wolf *The Lone Wolf will look familiar to anyone in sales. Lone Wolves are deeply self-confident. As a result, they tend to follow their own instincts instead of the rules. In many ways, the Lone Wolves are the 'prima donnas' of the sales force- the 'cowboys' who do things 'their way' or not at all. More often than not, they drive sales leaders crazy-they have no process compliance, no trip reports, no CRM (customer relationship management) entries... On average, Lone Wolves tend to do very well despite egregiously flouting the system because if they didn't do well, they'd probably have been fired already.*

The Reactive Problem Solver *The reactive problem solver is highly reliable and very detail oriented. While every rep in one way or another is focused on solving customer problems, these individuals are naturally drawn to ensuring that all of the promises that are inevitably made as part of a sale are actually kept once that deal is done. They tend to focus very heavily on post-sales follow up, ensuring that service issues around implementation and execution are addressed quickly and thoroughly.*

The Challenger *Challengers are the debaters on the team. They've got a deep understanding of the customer's business and use that understanding to push the customer's thinking and teach them something new about how their company can compete more effectively. They're not afraid to share their views, even when they're different and potentially controversial. Challengers are assertive-they tend to 'press' customers a little- both on their thinking and around things like pricing. And as many sales leaders will tell you, they don't reserve their Challenger mentality for customers alone. They tend to push their own managers and senior leaders within their own organizations as well. Not in an annoying or aggressive manner, mind you- then we'd simply have to call this profile 'the Jerk'- but in a way that forces people to think about complex issues from a different perspective.*

The CEB wanted to answer this primary question "Of all the things a sales rep could do well, which ones actually matter most for sales performance?" Their data pointed to on incontrovertible conclusion, the challenger sales style was significantly superior to any of them with an advantage of from fifty to one hundred percent over competing sales styles. A full description of the sales tactics used by the challenger salesperson is beyond the scope of this book, but unsaid is how they implicate business networking. To teach a company something new means to give them something new, and that means leveraging one's business networks to help provide it. But is this a hard and fast lesson of the challenger model? For the authors of the Challenger perspective and its literary representation in the book 'The Challenger Sale', this question is unanswered.

The Challenger 'Challenge'

The challenger model is data driven, and derives from the data, and not some preconceived notion of how sales should work. Indeed, if the data demonstrated that cold calling and reciting brochure information was the best approach in sales that would have been the sermon. Nonetheless, the challenger model may not be correct. Data models after all reflect correlations, not explanations, and the challenger data were generated for a for profit entity, the Corporate Executive Board, and do not appear in any peer reviewed journal that would have been a better guarantor of objectivity. In spite of this limitation, the Challenger model is a huge step up from the great mass of sales books and systems that derive from anecdotal, testimonial, literary or other evidence that is at best highly unreliable. The Challenger model most clearly argues for an explanatory sales style that synthesizes the customers' needs and addresses them in a new and comprehensive way that by definition must provide a challenging perspective to the client. That of course conforms to our own explanatory perspective towards business networking. However, this convergence also underscores the Challenger model's main weakness, not that the model is wrong, but that it is incomplete.

Keeping up with the Jones'

Behavioral Contrast: Keeping up with the Jones' is a tough thing to do, and is motivated by, well, the Jones'. This behavioral contrast represents the fact that the goodness of any behavior is not measured by absolute but by relative measures. That is, it hurts when you see other people having bigger cars, fancier houses, and neater lawns than you. So, to alleviate all that hurt, we try to outdo them in the materialism department, and thereby shift to them our pain, which is temporary anyways since the pain returns with our credit card bill. Behavioral contrast is the reason we are motivated to accumulate more and more stuff, when what we should be doing is build higher fences.

The Challenger sale goes beyond the mere recitation of features and benefits to actually challenge the customer or 'put them on the spot', and actually agree with your solution or look foolish. Naturally, you do this tactfully and respectfully, but nothing puts them more on the spot as explaining away why a rejection of your solution will in hindsight make him look dumb. Of course, with your wisdom and advice, you can remedy that.

It all has to do with making them aware of the broader opportunity costs of seizing the opportunities that your competitors are taking and will take at your expense. To illustrate this, consider this true example from a parallel universe. Consider a brilliant software engineer by the name of Andy Roid. He has developed a new operating system called 'ice cream popsicle' that can be installed on a small hand held computer with a tiny screen. The software will allow the little device to make phone calls, play music, access the internet, and run applications. Andy brings this to the attention of Bill, CEO of Microsponge, a world leading software company, but does not mention that other companies are taking note of such applications. Bill examines the software, lauds it and then dismisses it. Who would want such a thing he says, when we have pc's with big twenty five inch screens?

Three years later, Andy returns with a new version of his software called 'Sloppy Joe Sandwich' that is full of new and compelling features. Andy however does not inform Bill that his arch competitor Crapple will soon introduce similar software on a new hand held computer. Bill again admires the software, and again dismisses it as something no one would possible want.

Frustrated, Andy returns two years later with his newest OS, called 'Dill Pickle'. Now that Crapple's product is taking the market by storm, Bill wants to buy the new OS. Sadly, it was too late, as in his despair he made the product open source, and had given it away for free.

The Grass is always greener...

Andy relied on the features and benefits of his software when what really sold was knowledge about what his competition was up to. This contrast represented the opportunity cost to Microsponge that it was late to see. Opportunity costs don't cost until one gains sight of any opportunity lost. What Andy failed to do was lower the fence so that Bill could see what he was missing. What Bill needed was the big picture, not the little one, or in his case, a handheld one. Andy didn't press Bill on his perspective beyond a mere appraisal of his software's features, and he lost the sale because of it. He didn't teach Bill anything new that highlighted a loss due to his indecision. Without it, Bill was more indecisive than he would have been had he known the broader details.

A Unified Sales Principle

The problem with the Challenger model is that it is only half a model. After all, salespeople must know how to obtain leads and appointments, not just know how to handle themselves when they get them. Indeed, to get appointments that aren't otherwise handed to him by the marketing department, the challenger personality must be a split personality, with the hard worker sales type rising to the occasion to make interminable cold calls, the relationship builder using his cozy relationships to scare up referrals, or the lone wolf scrounging for leads in his own inscrutable and eccentric style. The irony however is that the challenger sales presentation contains the seeds of future referrals, as the invariable expansion of the customer conversation to provide wide-ranging solutions to a client should include products and services of individuals in one's private network. That information can of course be 'monetized' through co-referrals from your colleagues who presumably will engage the same challenger sales style. In other words, the challenger sales style is also a challenger *referral style* because compared to other sales styles, the challenger must make far more referrals to his vars and social vars to be successful. The key however is for the salesperson to set up her social vars with the same care as she sets up her regular vars. That of course not only requires persuasion, but also proof. Although this author hopes that he has attained to some small degree the former, the latter is indirectly supported by the challenger sales model, whose structure is predicted and advocated by the logical necessity and importance of the social VAR as a source of leads. In other words, the social VAR model of networking not only predicts the success of a challenger sale model, but *requires* it to succeed. So, we have come full circle, with how you sell determining how you get leads, and vice versa. Salesmanship and lead generation can only be combined if salesmanship and lead generation are not separate but self-reinforcing or synergistic. This unified sales principle thus becomes an empirically supported 'level playing field' that all sales reps may use, and may perhaps replace the Pareto Principle with one that makes all sales people more equal participants in sales success.

Although the science of sales is logically determined by how we determine and arrange incentives, incentives are not just logical but affective things. They influence emotions that determine not only the behavior of your client, but the behavior of the salesperson as well. As we will see in Part II of this book, fail to understand them and your effectiveness as a sales person will be significantly reduced or come to naught.

Chapter 5

Chamber Made

A Simple Guide to Business Networking in the Chamber of Commerce

The tactics of networking derive from a sound understanding of the social dynamics that drive behavior, but if you understand them from the insight gleaned from hard experience, the strategy of networking becomes a lot simpler, and it's easier to see how it can affect your bottom line. Networking, like fishing, requires the right fishing hole to find the right and willing partners for your networking success, and that is indisputably found in the networking events organized by your local Chamber of Commerce. Although other professional groups can arguably provide better forums for education, business lobbying, socializing, or community service, the Chamber is alone in not only emphasizing business networking, but in providing many different venues *for* networking. Because of this, *to succeed in business networking, Chamber membership is essential*. However, if you are going fishing for referrals and leads, you need to understand the rules of networking, and that is something the Chamber does not provide. The results are predictable. Individuals show up for Chamber networking events, meet a few people, and with scant networking success, stop attending Chamber functions. This is detrimental for the Chamber as new members become less likely to renew their membership, and visitors are far less likely to join. This results in Chamber membership not growing at the rate it should, with many potential members lost to groups like BNI which are far more unabashed in their emphasis on networking.

Regardless of the Chamber's limitations as a teaching forum, you at least know how to date, and that is precisely how networking works. Like dating, you meet someone in an inviting social setting who complements your interests. You ask them out, see them often, and instead of trading tokens of affection, you trade business information that leads to sales. Simple enough, and to outline how simple it really is, consider the hypothetical case of Bart, the manager of a computer services company. Bart is new in town, and wants to ideally meet a software developer, telephony rep, web site designer, or other complementary professionals who are well connected and are interested in the prospect of trading referrals. He begins with this action plan, and the Chamber will be the tool that allows him to succeed.

Business and Breakfasts

The first thing he does is search out the 'business and breakfast' or 'speed dating' events that are commonly held by the chamber. In these events, all attendees announce themselves, trade business cards and stories about themselves in round robin sessions. The attendees are there to promote their businesses, and Bart singles out two or three attendees who represent professions that strongly complement his service. He sets up a meeting with each of them at the event, and explains to them his interest in establishing a private network wherein they could meet frequently for the purpose of trading information, leads, referrals, and perhaps arranging joint calls to their common pool of clients. Since the network is better served if all members meet together rather than separately, Bart establishes a commonly agreed meeting time and protocol. Bart may start with a private network of two or three, but may later wish to grow the group by adding other professionals who have complementary interests. He can recruit them from the Chamber b and b, but another appealing venue for him and his colleagues are the far more common Chamber 'After Hours' business socials.

'After Hours' Business Socials

Unlike the b and b, Chamber business socials are not solely business networking affairs, as members and guests may use the functions for socializing, information gathering, or just hanging out. All of these purposes are incoherent with successful networking, and it becomes difficult to mingle in the group for lack of formal introductions and the fact that you do not know the purpose of each attendee you meet. Because of this, it is better to attend a business social with members of your own private network to work the group in concert. This facilitates meeting the individuals you can add to your network and those who are looking for services that your network can provide. Since you of course advocate the Chamber as you network in the crowd, you can increase your success markedly if the Chamber 'deputizes' you to do so as a Chamber Ambassador.

Chamber Ambassadors

Chamber Ambassadors are the deputized volunteer agents of the Chamber, who greet and introduce new guests, help at Chamber functions, and are charged with meeting present Chamber members at their place of business to advocate for the Chamber. This has many advantages for Bart, as he now can more aggressively introduce himself to Chamber members and to each other. In addition, Bart can meet other Chamber members in their place of business, and establish the social ties that he can later leverage into successful sales calls.

Having now established himself in the Chamber as an active member, volunteer, and advocate for Chamber success, Bart's networking effort has resulted in the growth of his business. Now Bart wants to meet higher-level decision makers who may not attend inexpensive Chamber socials. He opts instead for meeting business leaders at formal business lunches.

Formal Business Lunches

Since Bart wants to meet captains of industry rather than captains of the local bowling league, he wants to attend events that bowling league types cannot afford or do not find appealing. These are the business lunches that usually feature a distinguished speaker from the business, political, or educational community who the attendees may have interest in hearing. These are the settings where Bart can meet business leaders and decision makers who matter, if he can spare the cost and time. If Bart has a lot of time on his hands and wants the opportunity to network with a lot more people in high places, he joins a Chamber committee.

Chamber Committees

Chamber committee members focus on fulfilling the essential mission of the Chamber. Committees exist to further the higher goals of the Chamber such as education, lobbying, community service, and business development. By being a member of a Chamber committee, Bart can help drive the agenda of the Chamber by helping to improve Chamber events, serve the community, meet a lot of business leaders, and be 'paid' through the invaluable connections he is making that can eventually lead to sales.

So, there you have it, the short and simple way to business network, courtesy of the Chamber. Now there is a lot more to networking than this, but the essentials to any important concept from disease to rocket flight, can be explained simply, and with a little thought be used to derive equally simple procedures that work. For networking success, it's the little procedures that count.

Part II

The Behavioral Economics of Business and Social Networks

Chapter 6

The Affective Network

A Dismal Science

Behavioral economics studies the effects of social, cognitive, and emotional factors on the economic decisions of individuals and institutions and the consequences for market prices, returns, and resource allocation. The fields are primarily concerned with the bounds of rationality of economic agents.....(In other words, behavioral economics studies why regular economics does not work, or when in spite of all those great incentives to be good and productive, we still waste time surfing the web and otherwise goofing off.)

People are not robots, and their distinctly un-machinelike behavior is due in large measure to that fact that we have feelings, whereas robots don't. Feelings are always present in our lives, and may be lifted, depressed, hurt, energized, or be described by any of a score of metaphors. The problem is that describing what something is like does not describe what it *is*, and incorporating feelings into a logical model for decision making, or in the large, economic behavior doesn't work because economists don't know at root what feelings are. That's the problem with 'behavioral economics', which expands the mandate of economics from the logical to the emotional, and makes economic logic fuzzy, and it sensibility as dismal as before.

Economics is essentially the study of how incentives change behavior, *but it is not informed by a theory of motivation that is grounded to how our brains actually work.* This is a remarkable fact, and makes economics more akin to medieval medical practice that was at root clueless as to how human bodies worked. The answer quite simply is to define how incentive arouses and embodies affect or emotion, and to ground it to actual processes in the human brain. The fine details of such a neural or 'bio-behavioral' based definition of incentive motivation is beyond the scope of this book, and is left for a larger discussion in the appendix of this book. Nonetheless, its outline is simple, and is critical for our understanding of how business and social networks motivate behavior. As we will demonstrate, whether we are in network heaven or hell, along with the behavior and accompanying good or bad feelings that accompany them is all a matter of arranging and defining incentives right, and *timing* is the key.

Network Heaven

Following the rules mentioned in the preceding chapters, with the doubtless addition of a lot more of your own, you are now in network heaven. Like all heavens, everybody's available and they sure want to get in touch, which heaven being heaven is granted instantly. Everyone in your social and business networks needs a minute of your time, preferably now, and like a careening human pinball, everyone flips you about your personal space since you are now infinitely in touch. Email is one way, although voice mail, social media, internet news feeds join. Snail mail sadly is for those in the 'other' place. Got client, prospects. VAR's, friends, co-workers, or supervisors? They will be in touch often, unpredictably, and given your internet mobility, anywhere.

So, what's the price? Believe the hype and the ads and there is none, save for monthly bandwidth fees. But there is a price, subtle yet severe, that as we will demonstrate (if it is not already self-demonstrated) costs you a major portion of your day, reduces significantly your ability to attend to your job, and causes a lot of stressful misery. This price is the endless self-imposed distraction that keeps you from doing your job well and creates stress and endless regret. You may ask that if this is network heaven, then get me to that other place.

Who said this was heaven?

Network Hell

Welcome to the 'other' place.

To return to our farmer's market, Bob, Tom and Danielle of our little networking group certainly didn't think they were entering the networking underworld when they decided to modernize their barter network. Adding a few things like bar codes to track inventory in real time, frequent webinars, notices and email updates on the virtues of pumpkins, grapes, and apples, and of course the ability to text, chat, email and phone each of their partners would be a boon to productivity and an enticement to a better and friendlier relationship. Each of our partners would use this information wisely and well, or so it would seem.

Sadly, it was not to be. Bob, Tom and Danielle made sure they stayed in touch nearly all the time with each other and the progress of their present and hopeful business, creating a business milieu as distractive as it was productive. Now automated, their network created a cascade of seemingly infinite updates, all accessible immediately and all eliciting the 'want' to be accessed. And so, Danielle, followed in similar fashion by her partners, accessed her apple inventory not every day as she should but every ten minutes as she shouldn't. Multiplied by the constant contacts of her partners and peers and the minutiae of her business, the trivia of business shouldered aside the necessary facts needed to conduct a business, and her business faltered as her access to her business grew. Danielle ended the day regretful that she wasted so much of her days distracted, inattentive, and stressed.

So, what's going on here?

The greatest irony of the information age is that it allows us to create and bind together social and business networks of staggering variety and scope. But with this capability comes our ability to access continuous information updates of all possibilities, real and unreal. Information passes from one network connection to another at light speed, but it is the unpredictable *timing* of information that changes how we literally feel about our behavior in the moment, and these feelings never predict and often diverge from our long-term goals. As we shall see, when it comes to motivation timing is everything, and a surprising cue can motivate us to do the right thing, wrong thing, or   nothing at all.

Nature throwing us a curve

Go to any Wal-Mart, and you will see many human shapes and forms, all unremarkable and unnoticeable unless they cut in front of you at the register. If you want remarkable forms that are compelling (for men at least), you go to Rick's Cabaret, which will throw you a curve, lots of them. That human beings attribute emotional value to viewing or anticipating viewing different geometrical shapes points to how abstract properties of objects can determine value. The utility of an object is judged not by what it can do, but what it looks, smells, or tastes like. Humans respond to abstract properties of information that impinge upon our senses, from the smell of perfume to the melody of a song. We have to do so, because if not, our very survival would be at stake.

But there is another aspect of information that is subtle in nature, universal in scope, and without its presence, would render us as inert and lifeless as a floor lamp. It is the fact that we simply like, or should we say *want* to be surprised. It is nature's call, a 'seeking' or foraging instinct that drives us and all other creatures to seek out and experience new and surprising things. When we take a step in any path either real or virtual, we encounter and expect to encounter new and unexpected vistas. This to our forebears was the most important instinct, for without an urge to explore, we would be too stuck in a status quo that in a primeval world could change as fast as quicksilver, and unprepared, would consume us in a second.

Nonetheless, there is an intrinsic problem with our basic instincts, for by chasing the value of the curvature of a person's posterior these abstract values compromise our real or logical values. Similarly, by chasing the new we may often forego the good. But the new is often part of the good, thus making it difficult for us to separate them.

In times past we were lucky that our instincts were reined in by the simple fact that we could not readily indulge them. We had to wait a bit to for just the opportunity to be bad, and happenstance rather than effort made us virtuous. Virtue is a matter of delaying gratification, but if nature did the delaying for you, then it's pretty easy to be good. But if you cannot delay gratification, you must look to your understanding to keep your behavior in check. Social and business networks exist for gratification. After all, to succeed in business is to have success in life. Yet when we consider how incentives truly motivate behavior from the perspective of how our brains actually work, incentive motivation becomes something very different from the simple models of motivation that view people as rational actors who will always be motivated by rational goals. In other words, we are never, ever purely rational beings who will ever think straight, any more than, as we shall see, a car can ever drive straight.

Incentive Motivation

Automobiles never drive true. Take your hands off the wheel and you will veer very slightly or more to the right or left, so you keep your hands on to continuously correct for the car's logical misalignment with the road. But like a clock stopped at 12:00 being able to tell the right time two minutes a day, if you are turning right to conform with the car's tendency to veer right, the car is a well behaving machine that naturally points in the direction you want to go. Of course, if you wish to veer left than the car becomes cantankerous, and points to the direction opposite to where you want to go. This tendency makes every move adroit or maladroit if you are continually steering left or right, as when you ascend a winding road up a mountain while turning left, and down the mountain while turning right. Cars are logical despite the illogic, as our own logic intervenes to make them run true. So what does this have to do with human motivation or the 'drives' that make us move? For the psychological concept of incentive motivation, or how incentives motivate behavior, the desired object metaphorically 'pulls' you towards a goal. As a rule of thumb for behavior, this metaphor works in general fairly well, as people indeed are pulled one way or another dependent upon the rewards virtual and real scattered in front of them. This represents a 'rational actor' or utilitarian model for motivation, where people are driven by the predicted utility of behavior. However, as we discussed, humans are also motivated by an exploratory or 'seeking' instinct that gives momentary value to how information surprises us. This instinct is always 'on', is critical to sustaining motivation or behavior, and whether it coheres or is incoherent with the rational ends of our behavior it always moves our needle from behaving rational or true.

Dopamine

Dopamine: Neurochemical or 'master molecule of addiction' that controls or modulates the activity or 'firing' of arrays of brain cells, thus directing and 'fixing' attention by making attention either consciously or non-consciously have affective value or feel good. Since 99% of our time is spent waiting for or anticipating things, dopamine is nature's way of giving us a lollipop to sooth and reinforce the wait. Dopamine may also be called the master molecule of metaphor, since people are wont to assign any number of distinctive transcendent (e.g. higher consciousness, flow or peak experiences) or not so transcendent (e.g. cocaine high, mania) states to what amounts to a simple neuro-chemical fluctuation.

To understand how our complex bodies work, we resort to conceptual metaphor to make the complex seem easy, and to generate useful procedures. The persistent metaphor that describes human behavior is that we are utility maximizing creatures that respond more or less to rational rules. We are biological information processors, computer like, except for the fact our emotions or affect sometimes get in the way or help us on the way. The problem though is that affect always influences our behavior, and we often cannot recognize when it does. Nonetheless, the metaphor persists that we think like computers, and follow rational or logical principles to maximize our utility, both in the moment or in the future. In other words, the decision utility or present usefulness of behavior always matches its predicted utility or future usefulness. The moment-to-moment value of going to the store thus matches the value of being at the store. That is, until we run into something unexpected.

Consider your standard computer program. It always runs straight and true, until of course it malfunctions, freezes, or unexpectedly creates errors. It doesn't correct itself, the programmer does, who consciously is aware of what he has to do. As humans, if sustenance was a predictable thing, with nary an unpredictable pothole in the way, there would be no programmer ex machina, or need for conscious intervention from the cloud to set us straight. The brain has to do it itself, and to make sure it is conscious of what is important, it has evolved an unconscious sensitivity to information that mis-matches what otherwise is predicted. It is sensitive in other words to the error of its ways, or prediction error.

For any behavior, we are never sure that we will get to where we want to go in time. There will always be unexpected bumps in the road, delays or bypasses that obstruct or facilitate our progress. Experiencing or anticipating such unexpected events or prediction errors are correlated with positive (if the surprise is good) or negative (if the surprise is bad) affect. This emotional affect is brought to consciousness through the release or suppression of the neurochemical or 'neuro-modulator' dopamine in the mid-brain, which activates groups or arrays or nerve cells that accentuate learning, fix attention, and feel 'good' to boot. Think of the pleasant emotion you feel when you open a Christmas present, receive a party invitation, or even get a new email, and all represent the subjective aspect of dopamine in action. Similarly, when the present is poor, the party invitation is absent, and the email is never received, the subjective aspect of a reduction in dopamine is similarly felt. Finally, dopamine release scales or increases not only with the anticipated or experience discrepancy or surprise, but also with the importance or 'incentive salience' of that surprise. Thus we will be feel more 'excited' in anticipating a terrific Christmas present than an average one, and more depressed if that terrific present was not to be.

Dopamine is as critical to our understanding of motivation as our understanding of how microbes lead to disease. However, whereas we know the metaphors of disease and use them to effect procedures to get and stay healthy, dopamine has no easy metaphorical representations that can teach us how to behave in emotionally healthy and productive ways. Indeed, we don't know what quite to think about the good feelings that dopamine elicits except to naturally value a bit more the present behavior which correlates with it. As we shall see, this often causes mismatches between the value of behavior in the moment and its long-term value, with emotional and practical results both good and bad for our business and social lives.

So how can we incorporate this seeking instinct into our new model for behavior? We instinctively seek out positive surprises, but surprises depend upon how information is timed. If we know the timing of an event and can predict with certainly when and what events will occur, we are bored. However, if we cannot predict the timing, we are pleasantly aroused, energized and engaged. For networks, this is critical since social and business networks determine not just what information is traded but also how information is timed. The content of information is a *real* property of information, whereas the timing of information is an *abstract* property. Both determine the value of utility of behavior in the moment (or decision utility) but only the former determines value in the future (or predicted utility). How real or abstract properties cohere or diverge determines whether a network grows or collapses, and whether its members are happy and inspired, miserable and discouraged, or productive or non-productive. It all sounds complicated, but in actuality, it is simple. To illustrate, consider a network of two, an employee and his overseeing boss, performing a job that could be a pastime or merely an uncomfortable way to pass the time.

The Curious Case of Benjamin's Button Factory

Benjamin's button company is a hypothetical manufacturer of buttons, and a model employer. Each of Benjamin's employees contractually exchanges each button they make with a pull of a lever for a piece of the action. This piecework schedule rewards these industrious employees the most, as the more buttons you make the more you earn. This is all however completely predictable, and despite a high piecework rate, the engagement of his employees became piecemeal. Work was in other words boring, but was the boredom in the repetition, the sameness of the task, or just perhaps, in its timing?

In his wisdom, Benjamin changed the timing, making unpredictable the size of the reward for each pull of the lever. The reward could be zero or up to a hundred dollars, but the expected or average value of the average weekly salary would remain the same. He also made each employee aware of the 'winnings' of each other employee in the factory, with any alarm bell sounding when one hit on a lucky payout. To his immense gratification, the employees now pulled their levers like manic busy beavers. With employees so well satisfied, he was more comfortable on holding the line on salaries and benefits, since happy employees are less likely to leave.

Benjamin has 'gamified' the work process by changing the timing from fixed to variable and determined to indeterminate. He had in effect transformed his factory figuratively into a casino. In this case, abstract information, namely the timing of information relative to a reward, changed the value in the moment or the 'decision utility' of his employees' performance. Although the employees doubtless knew that their average compensation would almost certainly remain the same over time, they were more engaged and happier, and less inclined to strike for more wages and benefits to make amends to their boredom.

Inspired by his motivational gambit, Benjamin decided to change his figurative casino into literal one. The employees' average wages (or weekly winnings) were reduced to zero, but with free buffets and other comps added to comfort them in their impending poverty. Soon the Benjamin Button factory had not only satisfied workers, but a host of anxious applicants who wished to spend their odd hours also pulling levers. This he gladly accommodated with a new factory full of one armed machines that didn't make buttons at all, but accepted credit card donations from excited workers (or, make that players). The players weren't making anything, but they sure could be variably paid for their do-nothing behavior, even if the average payout over time created a dent in their savings, and an upward bump in Benjamin Button's bank account.

User screen for button making machine of the future

Benjamin's success came when he 'gamified' or changed the predictability and variance of the timing between behavior and awards.

Was this a good thing? It depends. Benjamin increased the satisfaction of his employees, but was it because he made them feel good and feel good about themselves or merely feel good? The former implies that the pleasure they feel while working extends to the pleasure they feel off the job when they consider their good work and what it implies for their families and friends. On the other hand, making the workplace more like a casino dulls the aspirations of workers to be adequately paid for the value they deliver. To Benjamin Button however, this was all academic, since gamifying the work place reduced his costs, increased employee morale, and because his employees suffered less boredom, he could afford to pay them less since he had no need to compensate them for their suffering, unless of course, his employees were salespeople.

The Curious-er Case of Benjamin's Button's Sales Manager

Even when for his employees' work was a drudge, Benjamin Button would never browbeat or insult them, unless of course they were unlucky enough to be in sales. Sadly, because of the nature of their craft, salespeople are subject to psychological tortures enviable by the CIA. Sales are often characterized by long lead times between effort and results. This results in long stretches of boredom and unavoidable lassitude punctuated with moments of frantic activity, enthusiasm when you make the sale, and terror or depression when you don't. It's all in a day's work, and unlike the button maker, no one sympathizes with you, because if you fail, it is all your fault.

Consider the sad life of Bart the salesman. Mike the sales manager gives Bart a list of hundreds of accounts from the phone book to cold call. Naturally, not many people want buttons, and fewer still want to meet or even talk to a button salesperson. Inevitably, although the rewards are great, the odds are long for a successful call, as Bart's calling behavior soon slows to a crawl as he hallucinates while counting ceiling tiles. Like the button factory worker, the momentary value of his behavior mismatches its long-term value, but in this instance, the sales manager is not so charitable to poor Bart, who can't find refuge in the safety of numbers that similarly bored coworkers can provide. So what is an enlightened sales manager to do? In a nutshell, he would follow the example of the factory manager, and instead of arranging high yet predictable incentives, he made them low to middling and unpredictable by following rules such as these:

Reward different aspects of behavior. There are many aspects of performance that contribute to sales, such as the number of cold calls, client visits, degree of product expertise and certification, presentation skills, etc. Reward them often, and sales will follow.

Mix hot leads with cold. Don't give hot leads for cold call performance, but integrate them with all calls. If not, performance will grind to a halt, no matter what enticing long term prospects you offer.

Do not contrast low with high performers. When we look to personal competition from tennis to chess, we want our competition to match our resources and skills, and be neither inadequate nor overwhelming. Similarly, publicly comparing your low performers to high performers will not encourage a competitive spirit but depression and resentment.

Give Encouragement Freely. Just be kind. Encouraging words are a better spur to performance than cruel and cutting remarks to employees. They know the standards that they are being held. Save the harsh remarks from when behavior needs correcting, not when it just needs to be motivated.

These recommendations integrate surprising positive information with performance, and elicit positive affect or 'good feelings' that can make an employee feel better about her work and keep her at her work. They all are integrated by management with the long-term goals of behavior that reflect excellent performance. However, there is another affective event that also changes a salesperson's performance, not just for the moment but also long term, until it quickly goes bad while you feel good and bad about it. The irony is, it is generally thought of as a good thing as it makes us unproductive and progressively drives us mad. It is distraction.

Distraction

"Say you look at information on a yearly basis, for stock prices or the fertilizer sales of your father-in-law's factory, or inflation numbers in Vladivostock. Assume further that for what you are observing, at the yearly frequency the ratio of signal to noise is about one to one (say half noise, half signal) —it means that about half of changes are real improvements or degradations, the other half comes from randomness. This ratio is what you get from yearly observations. But if you look at the very same data on a daily basis, the composition would change to 95% noise, 5% signal. And if you observe data on an hourly basis, as people immersed in the news and markets price variations do, the split becomes 99.5% noise to .5% signal. That is two hundred times more noise than signal —which is why anyone who listens to news (except when very, very significant events take place) is one step below sucker."

"To conclude, the best way to is to mitigate interventionism is to ration the supply of information, as naturalistically as possible. This is hard to accept in the age of the internet. It has been very hard for me to explain that the more data you get, the less you know what's going on..." Nicolas Taleb

----

Joachim: "They're requesting communications sir."

Khan Nooniem Singh (super intelligent tyrant and web master): "Let them eat static!" —Star Trek II, 'The Wrath of Khan'

Before the internet, information came and went like the timely arrival of a train. It arrived on time, gave you a pick me up, dropped you off, and left. If you wanted a stock market report, the local news, or letter from Aunt Alice, it all came at set times, was concise and short, and it left. You got what you really needed and little else, and then you moved on.

Nowadays, when you want information updates, you get what you need, and every variation of what you need, and you can and will stick around more than you should to consume it, even though its logical value to you rapidly diminishes to worthlessness. You can read about the stock market, the local news, and Aunt Alice's activities in seemingly infinite variations, shapes, and forms, and you can do it at any time. For our social and business networks, the situation is the same. Get a phone call from your boss, an email from a sales colleague, or an internet update on a new product feature from a vendor, and this new information will perk you up and help you do your work better. Unlike your 1960's counterpart however, the information does not leave, and stays in infinite novel variations to entice and entertain you. The result is that you end up even less productive than your information challenged ancestor.

Besides the invariable Twitter and Facebook feeds that are an obvious hindrance to productivity, we are decidedly ambivalent about the other information that we need, but don't need. This underscores the most important and most difficult of our recommendations, namely the complete avoidance of distraction, and in particular, the internet. Whereas it is easy to adopt a policy to provide unexpected positive updates or information to employees, distraction is much more difficult to manage. This is because distraction is in essence a changeling, and can rapidly morph from being useful (and non-distractive) to useless, and then back again. In contrast to unexpected positive information that business and social networks provide and can be engineered to provide, distraction generally does not begin as distraction, but as information that we need to do our work.

Get an email from your boss, a call from a vendor, an endorsement from a colleague on a social network, or just access stock market information from the web, and if they repeat themselves with minor variations in a follow up email, call, endorsement, or view, you are not being informed, but merely distracted. But is this a problem? It depends upon who you ask.

Internet providers, advertisers and social media give the impression that benefits are high and costs are low. This is a false. Google, Facebook and their ilk are in the distraction business, plain and simple. Their profitability would collapse if we accessed them when we needed them, not when we want to be stimulated by them. They exist to provide you all the information you need, but at the cost of all the information you want. A fair trade, until you realize that information can be a very toxic thing, and a threat to our physical and psychological well being.

Cold Calls

Study real hard goes the maxim, and you will go to Harvard. Likewise, make a thousand cold calls a week and you will make quota. The one is necessary to get a good job, the other is necessary to keep it. So why do these motivators fail? Both are predictable outcomes to supreme effort and of course a bit of inherent ability. But these excellent horizons are distant ones, and in the meantime you perceive your progress at a snail's pace, which is to say, no pace at all. There is in short nothing surprising when work is a boring drudge, no matter how bright the eventual outcome. So, you slow down and even stop, and not even the threat of a lost scholarship or job will motivate you.

A case in point is the dreaded cold call. Cold calls play by the odds. Make enough of them and like playing the lottery, something good will happen. Fortunately, even the lottery (or casino for that matter) knows that to keep you playing in search of the big prize, it is important to scatter a few small prizes along the way to keep your interest high. You need in other words a few side motivations to keep your eye on the ball. Call centers and boiler rooms know this, as 'pressure' from your co-workers or peers keep you moving. It is hard after all to hang up the phone and stare at the ceiling if your co-workers notice it. Unfortunately, the sales person is generally entrusted to make cold calls on his own, and too often fruitlessly fight the demotivating fact of a boring and all too predictable job.

Cold calls are good way to call them, because we inevitably freeze up when we make them. But it's not fear so much as the expectation of failure that is the cause for out reluctance to pick up the phone, and prospect list in hand, begin to grind out call after call to a quite willing collection of answering machines. Before voice mail and the internet, a cold call could get through if you could sweet talk a receptionist or so-called gatekeeper who would put you through to her boss who in his blissful ignorance would listen to your spiel. Nowadays, you can be the receptionist's best friend and your calls will still be routed to voice mail, and your message will be ignored even if you are rightfully warning against the apocalypse.

The problem for cold callers is the decline in the importance of voice mail for all calls, let alone the sales variety. Look to our own experience, when each email message takes a second to read, a few more to respond, and all archived and searchable until a google-plex years from now (that's one followed by 100 zeroes, or a blink in infinity, which means that God or the Google com-plex will probably be reading your emails in the distant future.) Compare that to a voice mail message, which is often longwinded, easily off point, is hard to transcribe, and is erased by the end of the day. Cold calls are best left to robots, who can talk with silent precision to other robots, leaving the customer blissfully unaffected, and you the salesperson ineffective.

A final problem with voice mail is that it is just plain boring. The monotony of repeating yourself from one call to the next does not endear itself to a lively and exciting day. Rather, your speed and precision fall off precipitously, and staring at the ceiling becomes more rewarding than dialing avidly to surpass a sales ceiling.

If you must cold call, set up a 'boiler room', or better yet, hire someone who will call for you who happens to work in a boiler room. Boiler rooms provide side motivation when forward motivation is not enough, and if you hire someone to do it for you, is invariably cheaper than if you had to do it yourself. Whether you do it or someone else, the motivation to cold call is the contrast of falling behind the efforts of your peers in plain view. Without group pressure your effort and effectiveness will rapidly fall off as you slump listlessly at the chair, staring at the ceiling.

A Note on Door-to-Door Cold Calling

Cold calls are meant to open doors, but with answering machines and the decline of its effectiveness due to the internet and email, open doors must literally be opened to get in touch with your prospect. Whereas phone call solicitation is declined through the friendly answering machine, there is no such robotic gatekeeper when you literally walk through the gate. You confront the old fashioned human type, who will take your card and information, and may throw you out or pass you to her supervisor, but never thankfully into voice mail limbo.

Walking through doors is not quite like being like the vacuum cleaner salesman of old. For one thing, a sales call has far more credence to a sales manager than a sales phone call, since you are actually meeting with people rather than pitching to a tape recorder. Secondly, you actually stand a chance of meeting with a decision maker, even though he may be glaring at you while pointing to the 'no soliciting' sign on the door. Third, it is a lot less boring than cold calling, and if teamed up with a fellow salesperson for a complimentary service, the tag team effect can actually make the door-to-door cold call fun.

Toxic Information

In the 1960's a popular slogan for Lay's Potato Chip's was uttered in a commercial by Bert Lahr (of cowardly lion fame): "bet you can't eat just one". Bert was right, you just can't eat one potato chip. Extend this motto to all the other compulsion-inducing events in our life from candy to pornography, and we recognize that our will power can't cut it when faced with all the good stuff we can eat, imbibe, or view that becomes a veritable and irresistible siren's song once we get a taste, whiff, or sight of it. So, what is the solution? **Don't snack**, and wait until a specific time if you must to indulge in these things, and even then, think twice before you do it. We time our indulgences because once sampled our indulgences take over our better reasoning, and we will have one more proverbial potato chip, and then another, and another. By consuming too much of anything, it can become 'toxic', and detrimentally influence our health, productivity, and peace of mind. Timing our temptations is a truism that most of us follow, except for the one indulgence that derives from timing itself: information. How information is timed doesn't seem to matter much, because after all, facts are just facts, and there's nothing addictive about plain old information, or is there?

Social and business networks present information and they time information, but they are ultimately dependent upon the tools they use that deliver it. Before the internet revolution, the arrival of information was for the most part timed due to the limitations of the delivery mechanisms that were then available. For a businessperson, reports on product sales, delivery, availability, billing, and general news came and went with the six o'clock news, daily newspaper, mail, and the weekly call report from a salesperson. Now we can receive them at any time, and in infinite variations, and all of it is something we want to access right now. On the flip side, this information gluttony is enough to make one feel, well, overloaded.

Information Overload Overloaded

Whenever there is a compelling crisis, there must be a compelling solution. If terrorists attack us, oil supplies are about to run dry, and our kids get peanut allergies, a cardinal rule is to let no crisis go to waste. So, we respond by invading a near eastern country, pass a law to turn half the corn crop into alcohol, and recall the entire U.S. peanut harvest to protect the folks.

The latest crisis that compels a massive response, or at least massive commentary, consulting, and punditry, is the crisis of 'information overload'. The concept of information overload applies to an overabundance of information that has uniform value and must be accessed and processed in the present. Because we are mentally unequipped to choose between all this stuff, and feel compelled to access it anyways, it drives us to distraction and causes inattention, regret, and stress, not to mention wasting gobs of our valuable time. Indeed, it has inspired think tanks to take to their stopwatches and observation booths to calculate its cost on our productivity, which goes down by almost a third and costs more than a trillion dollars annually.

Sounds to me like a real call to action, or at least for a lot of seminars, speeches, consultation sessions, and white papers, all available for you for a fee. The problem is, the concept is nonsense, and although real, the crisis is elsewhere. The fact is we have always had more information in front of us than we know what we do with. So what do we do? We follow our rules of thumb, the tried and true heuristics that can make good enough the best road to follow. We continually parse or filter information with no difficulty. Read a restaurant menu, and even though we realize we cannot sample all the dishes, we have no problem in choosing which entrees to consume, with helpful recommendations from the waiter of course. Similarly, experience a medical crisis with hundreds of people needing your aid, and you establish a medical triage to segregate out those people who can be helped, those who cannot, and those who can wait.

When we don't know the best choices, we can make arbitrary ones and live with them. However, if we *do* know the best choices, and fail to follow them, then there is a problem, and we end up conflicted, tense, and 'overloaded'. The overload metaphor conjures a boiler for a steam engine that is heating up and is ready to vent, or maybe explode. Like the evil computer that gets confused, steams up and blows up by the suasion of Captain Kirk who convinces it not of the error but the contradiction of its ways, our problem as organic computers is that we can't decide between doing the thing that feels good or the thing that feels right. Anxiety occurs when you thus cannot choose, even though you know what the best choices are. It's a siren's song when you are irresistibly lured against the rocks when you know that steering away is the better choice. That siren's song is affect.

Odysseus Tormented by the Sirens of Google

To be torn between being affective and being effective has no easy resolution, but it does have well documented problems that threaten our psychological and physical livelihoods. Primarily, we become regretful of a day misspent. Secondly, we are inattentive and unsuccessfully try to do multiple things as once, or multitask. Third, we become stressed by the incompatibility of these demands. All are events that should not be the bounty of a hard day's work. Nevertheless, as shall see, their remedy is simplicity itself.

Regret

Nine days after our departure from Troy my men and I found ourselves in a strange land and miles from our original course. In order to learn a bit more about this alien place, I sent three of my bravest soldiers on a scouting mission. Unfortunately, they learned a lot more than I had counted on. On their expedition, my men found themselves among natives of our temporary habitat. Like any good host, these natives introduced my men to one of their favorite appetizers: the lotus. A single taste of this native fruit made my soldiers forget everything they had ever known; where they were from, where they were going, everything. Although many of my other men would have enjoyed this easy way of living at this point, I decided I wouldn't give them the chance to choose it. It was for their own good, of course. –Homer's Odyssey

Win the Super Bowl and it is the stuff of pride and memory, however if we won a virtual Super Bowl courtesy of the Madden 14 video game, it is forgettable in an instant. Both can serve up the same thrills, but only the former can serve up the same memories, and it is memory that gives meaning and pleasure to life. The positive uncertain implications of events past can be 'relived', and in their afterglow, impart the same pleasures that occurred when we first experienced them.

Ultimately, to make choices that have meaning is important because of the importance of the continuity of good feelings or positive arousal. To *look forward* to an event means to emotionally ride upon the real or imagined implications of prospective future events, and to *reminisce* on the event means to relive it anew. If the events have no implications, as with information mediated by a distractive world, then meaning dies and we are left with ennui, depression, and despair as we contemplate our losses, or what could have been. Odysseus recognized this when he wrested his men from a land of infinite delights where meaning was absent. As our own delights approach a similar infinity in scope and meaninglessness, our personal liberty prevents a similar guiding hand,

and can be rescued only by our own guiding intelligence. But even our intelligence is at the mercy of choice, and as we will next note, if our wits as well as our hopes are dashed by the prospects of incommensurate or incompatible choices, then choice is doubly something to be wary of.

Distraction by the numbers

We underestimate the amount of time we lose to distraction. To demonstrate this, just take a measure how you apportion your time. Whether at home or at work, you'll probably come up with statistics similar to those accrued by the web consultant Jonathan Spira, who stopwatch in hand, found out how knowledge workers actually spent their time in such paragons of organization efficiency as Morgan Stanley, Intel, etc.

From his data and other sources, he produced these staggering statistics of time and money lost due to information overload, such as:

What Was I Working On Again?

Studies by Basex, a company that looks at workers' efficiency at information-intensive businesses, show that significant amounts of time are wasted by interruptions, like unimportant e-mail messages, and the time it takes to refocus on work.

HOW A TYPICAL INFORMATION WORKER'S DAY IS SPENT

28%	25%	20%	15%	12%
Interruptions by things that aren't urgent or important, like unnecessary e-mail messages — and the time it takes to get back on track.	Productive content creation including writing e-mail messages	Meetings (in person, by phone, video and online)	Searching through content, like the Web, digital communications and paperwork	Thinking and reflecting

Source Basex

THE NEW YORK TIMES

Information Overload cost the U.S. economy almost $1 trillion in 2010

A minimum of 28 billion hours is lost each year to Information Overload in the United States.

Reading and processing just 100 e-mail messages can occupy over half of a worker's day.

It takes five minutes to get back on track after a 30 second interruption.

For every 100 people who are unnecessarily copied on an e-mail, eight hours are lost.

58 percent of government workers spend half the workday filing, deleting, or sorting information, at a cost of almost $31 billion dollars.

66 percent of knowledge workers feel they don't have enough time to get all of their work done

94 percent of those surveyed at some point have felt overwhelmed by information to the point of incapacitation.

One major Fortune 500 company estimates that Information Overload impacts its bottom line to the tune of $1 billion per year.

All of this sounds really bad until you do a simple thought experiment, Shut down the internet, personal email communications, and other distractions except for one hour at eight am and one hour at six pm each day. You will find that information overload goes away, as you effectively return yourself to the good old days of the 60's when information was timed just so, with the added benefit that using internet filters, you can find what you need much faster and effectively than your counterpart of yesteryear.

Inattention

Multi-Tasking: *Rapid cognitive shifting between different simultaneous tasks that present you the gratifying illusion that you are doing twice as much when you are actually doing less in twice the time.*

To be distracted means to be inattentive. However, if distraction is an important thing, then we are still inattentive, but now we are 'multi-tasking', and thus can do two things at once. A splendid prospect, except for the fact that we generally end up doing two things badly, and end up worse than when we started.

Moving from one task to another is an easy thing if they are all related to the goal at hand, but if they are not, then you are multi-tasking. Multi-tasking means to attempt to do multiple dissimilar behaviors simultaneously, or to rapidly shift between multiple dissimilar behaviors. The distinction is that these behaviors serve *dissimilar* ends. For example, task shifting while building a house entails different behaviors that serve a singular end, namely constructing a house. However, the carpenter is multi-tasking if he talks on the phone *while* constructing the house. For our personal lives, the rapid growth of near instant communication between members of our business and social networks has attended prevalent task switching between different channels of information that serve different goals, with an attendant research literature that has demonstrated how multitasking adversely impacts attention, memory, and cognitive efficiency.

Studies have consistently demonstrated that people show severe disruption in their productivity when even very simple tasks are performed at the same time, especially if both tasks require selecting and producing action[1][2]. For example, it is difficult, and likely impossible to learn new information while engaging in multitasking[3]. Similarly, students who engaged in more multitasking reported more problems with their academic work[4]. These results demonstrate a common-sense observation, namely that executive attention is a fixed resource, and if it is subdivided, less is available for individual tasks, and competence suffers. In the present day, information systems afford us the opportunity either to do many different tasks simultaneously, or to rapidly switch back and forth between tasks. *Multi-tasking* means doing several tasks simultaneously, whereas as a sub-type of multi-tasking, *task-switching* means to rapidly alternate between several tasks. Does either way suffice to make us more productive, efficient, and intelligent?

Well, no. Even if multi-tasking did not directly result in cognitive impairment, it still would make nervous and stressed, which at least indirectly impairs our ability to act and think.

In work environments, 28% of a typical knowledge worker's time is spent in engaging or recovering from non-productive distractions.[5] This means that for those business managers trying to squeeze out productivity by giving disparate work to simultaneously do (e.g. answering the phone while working on a project), employees end up doing less. Passing from the anecdotes of personal experience, the research literature demonstrates that multi-tasking also strongly correlates with stress. For example, Workers who are juggling interruptions are significantly more stressed and frustrated than those who are not interrupted[6]. When given a "job" answering e-mail, they experienced significantly more stress and frustration when frequently interrupted. This generally underscores the obvious, as we generally do feel stressed when we have to balance several dissimilar tasks at the same time. What is less obvious is that continuous task switching has not often been associated with tension and stress, but to something else.

Stress

Stress: Instinctive reaction comprised of muscles tensing, adrenaline percolating, and blood rushing from head to foot in preparation for fighting or taking flight. Stress is a hardwired response that evolved from our caveman days when we had to constantly run from hungry dinos and saber tooth tigers. This explains why we get stressed out when deciding what shirt to buy, and why we get bent out of shape when we notice that the other line in the bank or grocery store is moving faster. Of course, if you buy into this explanation, then something else is rushing from head to foot, namely your common sense.

It all has to do with our ancestors making do in a dangerous world. Often they had to make a run for it, as lions, tigers, bears and other assorted Paleolithic threats pressured them to make quick decisions to fight or make flight. Over time, nature found a way to make this decision a bit more automatic and a lot faster, and through evolution's graces, the stress response was born. Of course, nowadays, we only proverbially have to put up our dukes or make a run for it, nonetheless, if we have a stressful day on the job, we blame that evolved biological connection between unbearable demands and an ancient bear bearing down.

The is picaresque story to be sure, and is repeated ad nauseam by any expert type who has a quick word to say about the subject. There is only one problem. For our daily stresses, this is not true. When we encounter a real threat in the wild we become psychologically primed for action. Our heart races, hormones flow, and blood courses to our limbs with muscles tensed and primed for action. So what happens when we are faced with the irreconcilable demands of a stressful day? Our posture changes, or rather our postural muscles or musculature activate or tense. Postural muscles are the muscles that literally hold us up. They keep us from falling over, not running fast, hardly a necessary trait it seems for a 'flight or fight' response.

Stress is often thought of as a reaction to demand, any demand. The definition is hardly fitting when the 'demand' is a walk on a beach, a trip to the movies, or a date with your wife. A better definition for stress comes from those demands that we can't act upon without losing something important in return. In other words, the problem is not with demand, but with difficult choices, or dilemmas. The dilemmas we normally face however are not the life or career threatening one's that face us periodically, but the small inconsequential dilemmas that we face continually. It is sweating the small stuff, the results of the stresses that confront us daily, and are best illustrated through the example of a beloved fairy tale character.

The Cinderella Effect

Cinderella Effect: Lightly clench your fist, now keep it clenched for 15 minutes. At first, you will feel nothing, but as time goes on your muscles will tire and give out, and this otherwise innocuous behavior becomes quite painful. It sounds dumb, but we unconsciously do this all the time. Whenever a muscle or group of muscles are tensed and stay tensed, they will soon give out and recruit other muscles to literally take up the slack, resulting in an equally literal pain in the neck. Also known as a syndrome of accepting your current lousy situation, or in other words, like Cinderella, if the slipper fits, wear it.

It's not the lions, tigers, and bears, it's just that your muscles are worn out from a hard day at work. Cinderella knew this at the end of a particularly hard day, which given her fairy tale status (as well as for many of us who don't live in fairy tale worlds) was every day. Her misery was not due to heavy lifting, but a lot of non-stop lifting, and sweeping, and washing, and so on of the sort that didn't build her up but ground her down.

So how did this happen? Isn't activity good for you? When our muscles tense, they give out, and a runner, weight lifter or athlete must take a time out, catch one's breath, and let her muscles relax. In Cinderella's case, her muscles were active all the time, with scant time for recovery. But these weren't the type of muscles that when used give you a good workout and a better physique. It was her postural muscles, also aptly named 'Cinderella' muscles that were activated most, and their activity does not work out your cardiovascular system but rather wears it out. These are the muscles that when continually activated cause pain and exhaustion, and they are set in motion by the continual choices we make between minor events. However, the problem is like drinking a refreshing glass of sea water, we don't know we've done wrong until it's too late, or maybe not at all.

Stress and Seawater

We all know or should know that salt water doesn't quench thirst, it makes it worse. But to the uninformed, when you drink it, it hits the spot, then after a few minutes you become even more thirsty. It would be a bad move to go right back to the ocean for a second drink, and without a good explanation why that would not be a good idea, you would probably do it[2]. The reason of course is that the bad effects of drinking salt water happen some minutes after you drink it, so it's difficult to connect the dots and attribute much of your thirst to salt intake rather than a sunny day.

The seawater metaphor fits our own experience with stress, as we often take time off from time to time from a high-pressure environment not to sit back and meditate or rest quietly, but to pursue a few non-stressful and interesting pursuits like checking our social media accounts, internet news feeds, or other diversions. The problem is, the interesting or stimulating aspect of these diversions prime you to look forward to them (just like snacking during the day causes you to be tempted to snack even more during the day) with pleasurable anticipation during business hours, and that forms a continuous choice or contrast between what you could be doing and what you *should* be doing. This contrast correlates with the tensing of your postural musculature, which gives out rapidly and recruits other muscles to pick up the slack, resulting in a literal pain in the neck and resulting stress. So, the relaxing time you spend surfing around the internet during a time out to avoid stress ends up *causing* stress because it acts to emotionally prime you to expect to give in to distraction throughout the day, causing a continuous dilemma. However, like our ignorant seawater drinker, *it can be too easy to attribute*

---

[2] In fact, you can drink seawater without ill effect if you mix a little of it with regular water. Seawater has a salinity of about 35 g/kg. Blood has a salinity of about 9 g/kg. Therefore, if you mix one part seawater with anything greater than three parts fresh water, the mixture is potable.

the resulting tension and stress to aspects of the job rather than aspects of the time out, and we end up imbibing ever more on Facebook to salve our nerves when it may be Facebook and not our job that is causing most of the stress!

So, what is the solution? Well, the stress gurus have the procedure right, but not the explanation. You really *do* need to time out from stress, and resting rather than web surfing is the way to go. The key is to explain why although timing out with Espn.com is the pause that refreshes, in the long term it is the pause that can kill.

Network Hygiene

If we begin to eat a juicy apple, and after a few seconds, it begins to get rancid, we stop eating the apple because it tastes disgusting. That's nature's way of enforcing dietary hygiene. On the other hand, if we are eating a food that is bad for us in the long term, like a bowl of potato chips, we keep eating. That's because nature, or the elementary brains bestowed upon us and our animal cousins by nature, are only good at detecting the short-term value of the things we consume. We can compensate for this by our ability to think (thanks to a nifty brain add-on called the neo-cortex), but nonetheless our thinking part (chips are bad) tends to conflict with the affective part (chips are tasty), and we end up regretful and stressed. This position can be resolved by resolving to only eat potato chips at set places or times.

Similarly, consuming novel and positive information is good for us until it quickly becomes rancid, but we keep consuming it because it feels good, even though we know that long term it is not good for us. Again, we are conflicted, and end up regretful, distracted, and stressed. The problem is, we don't realize this, and like the tobacco companies of old, our internet providers from Google to Facebook and its advertising partners are incented to keep us from applying the internet hygiene that can save our minds and maybe our souls. The only thing that can save us, as it did tobacco smokers of the past, are good and sound metaphors that describe what internet hygiene is.

Personal hygiene is a simple thing, once you understand the right metaphors that act as proxies for the real explanation as to how our bodies work. Eat veggies, avoid sweets and meats, exercise regularly, and always wash your hands before you eat. To make the explanation for these behaviors stick, we need to use the metaphors of germs, cholesterol, vitamins, and cardio-vascular conditioning to justify them. For the concept of incentive motivation, I have introduced a new metaphor, that of the seeking response, that when coupled with our metaphorical representation of the neurochemical dopamine and our standard concepts of utility or reward, describes how human interactions within networks motivate. This new perspective on incentive motivation does not just describe how specific practices in sales work or don't work, it *explains* them. Cold calling, sales contrast, and even small intermittent kindnesses all have their special advantages and disadvantages in social and business networks that derive from primary principles of human motivation that are easy to understand.

As I have demonstrated, timing in networks is everything, but humans far overestimate their ability to master and control it. They in other words are subject to mistimed or distractive information that affects their performance, intelligence, and mental health. Modern business and social networks and the information networks that support them have moved the responsibility for information timing to the individual, and the individual cannot handle it. So, what is the solution? Simply do what we do when we encounter other events that have highly addicting qualities, quarantine them to a separate time and place. It applies in equal measure not just to individuals, but also to individuals in their social and professional networks. If your colleague, coworker, or boss insists on distracting you, and you can't avoid them, the following advice can only be useful if they follow it as well.

Chapter 7

Game of Networks

The Knob of Motivation

As we have noted, effective networking is impaired by distraction, but it is nonetheless quite hard to resist distraction. Better to make your present activity a whole lot more important. After all, who has time to waste and would want to waste time when faced with deadlines and assorted other demands that keep us fixed on our primary tasks? As we have seen through our observation of our hypothetical button factory, if not calibrated right, demands can make performance boring, stressful, and depressing. The question is how can we avoid the negative aspects of demand and use demands to make work more interesting, fulfilling, and fun while keeping you and your firm's interests squarely in sight? The answer is that it comes from a lot more demands from everywhere, all timed and mediated by business and social networks. The more interest and enthusiasm that can be elicited, the better, but ultimately it is the network that counts.

If we were in possession of a metaphorical knob we could turn to ramp up our motivation at will to pursue the important things in our lives, we would likely temporarily elect to turn it up not modestly but all the way. For one thing, it feels better that way, and it assumes our absolute attention to our important tasks. Our workday would be characterized by a singular enthusiasm and focus on our job, with a similar dedication to spouse, children, and self-improvement that would not cease at the end of the working day. Feeling good would overmatch even the modest advantages of being good, as our momentary pleasures do not inform us about how good the result of our behavior really is. In this way, our momentary affect has a way a taking us away from a needed time out, vacation, or other break where we can 'smell the flowers'. Nonetheless, that is but a small price to pay for the prospects of success. We want to be not just interested in but *obsessed* with doing a good job, learning an important skill, and being a great friend, parent, or spouse, and networks and only networks can take us there. If we can do so by the informed management of our networking environment, so much the better.

Effective networks are gamified networks, because supreme accomplishment depends upon obsession and the positive affect that drives it. Where do we find this positive affect? It comes from the uncertainty that derives from games. But first, we need to explain what a game is.

Gamification

Hard Wired: *Tiny little, yet hard wires that cause us to like sex, be afraid of spiders, and prefer vanilla ice cream. Hard wires are an essential ingredient for our behavior that dispenses with the need for hard thinking.*

Game: *The act of having a good time while wasting time.*

Gamification: *The act of having a good time while investing time. When the investment has a negative (for you) return, gamification may also mean to exchange your time or money for a token, nudge, wink, like, or badge that has no monetary or otherwise practical value to you but rather to someone else, with the belated recognition that you don't need any 'steenking badges'.*

What's a game? First, let's have the incomplete definition, courtesy of Wikipedia. "*A **game** is structured playing, usually undertaken for enjoyment and sometimes used as an educational tool. Games are distinct from work, which is usually carried out for remuneration, and from art, which is more often an expression of aesthetic or ideological elements.*"

The problem with this definition is that it doesn't define what 'structured' is, and it doesn't define how and why positive affect or enjoyment is elicited, how it rises and falls, how it changes motivation, learning, and attention, and how it is reflected in the activity of the human brain. It also errs by separating from games the monetary and personal remuneration we get from our business and social networks from participating in games, which as I will demonstrate also comes from games. Finally, it does not consider how merely watching a game can be as rewarding as playing a game. Correcting for this, I offer a hopefully better and more succinct definition.

Complicated version: A game is the continuous elevation of decision utility through a present or anticipated timing variance that provides continuous and high positive prediction error and corollary positive affect. **Simple version: a game is a continuous positively uncertain task that makes the task fun.** Complicated version: Gamification is the matching or overmatching of decision utility with the predicted utility of future dependent outcomes through the employment of continuous positive prediction error. **Simple version: gamification is a game married to a positive long-term outcome.** Both the timing variance and value of the predicted outcome determine resulting affect that is governed by the activity of midbrain dopaminergic systems, or biochemical activity in the human brain that correlates with focused attention, heightened learning, 'energy', and 'pleasure'. This activity in turn is elicited by the perception or anticipation of surprising act-outcome discrepancies, or novelty, as well as the degree of importance of the goal of behavior. Finally, a game is rewarding as a task that is performed by an individual or as a performance by others that is observed. For example, football players are rewarded by playing the game, and football spectators are similarly rewarded by watching the game.

To illustrate, consider a simple deck of cards. If you were to consciously arrange them in different patterns representing suit or rank, manipulating a card deck would be a predictable and boring affair. However, establish a set of rules for the ordering of the cards that make the moment-to-moment predictability of successfully completing the task variable, and we in effect have created value from nothing. Finally, increase the value of successfully completing the game by a monetary reward, trophy, or other emblem of success, and affect rises in tandem. In other words, it just feels better, and not only for the player, but also for the individuals watching the game itself.

Motivation from a Deck of Cards

Behavior can be a game if it leads to no goal or it can be gamified if it leads to a tangible goal. Sometimes that goal is practical, such as completing your job better and faster, with pleasure and without stress. In this case, you are rewarded with monetary tokens. However, gamification can also occur if no monetary reward is attained, as in winning a chess match, but with the token award of the regard of your friends, peers, or the public at large.

Games are typically looked upon as trivial, or distinct from important activities like work. However, the opposite is the case. Games are necessary to *do* work. Just ask our really distant ancestors. For animals, life is unpredictable, and thus potentially dangerous, so evolution favored creatures that could attend and deal with it. To cope with unpredictability, you had to seek it out and make it predictable and safe. Unpredictable events could be experienced in the wild as when a creature forages for food or fight to win a mate, or they could be modeled as when creatures play. The need to make the unpredictable predictable is necessary for animals to survive, including the human one. It is in our nature to seek out unpredictability, particularly if it is mated with a higher and future purpose. The higher the purpose, the greater the affect or 'pleasure'. We are in other words 'hard wired' to be attracted to games or gamified environments, with an inborn preference for games that have meaning. The only problem is that our notion of what games and gamification mean is faulty.

Gamification Gamed

Gamification is the newest buzzword to describe how manipulating the timing of information can raise interest, engagement, and pleasure. Gamification is problematic however because it is predominantly emblematic. Gamification is about using the emblems of games, such as badges, scores, levels, rankings, etc. to match and reinforce performance aspects of a local task, but without considering how tasks are concurrently motivated by the uncertain feedback mechanisms embedded in our personal networks. As usually defined, gamification stays within the confines of the task, and does not consider the dependency of gaming behavior to the equally uncertain information provided by our business and social networks.

Gamification is merely a collection of procedures found commonly in games that are used to motivate behavior to achieve ends that benefit you, or more commonly, the entity that designed the game for you. It is procedural and not explanatory in nature, and because of this does not integrate its procedures with the laws of affect deduced from an analysis of how our behavior derives from our brains 'in action'. Specifically, it is not informed by a sound neurologically based understanding of how incentive motivation works. This has resulted in a host of misconceptions about what gaming is and how games can be gamified to achieve higher ends. These are:

Conflation of feedback and discrepancy- Feedback represents information on performance progress, and may be from moment to moment (as when you are walking to the door) or intermittent (when you receive your bank account statement). Feedback may also be surprising or completely expected, and motivating and energizing on the one hand and de-motivating and boring on the other. So to say that people respond to feedback is meaningless, since it is an aspect of feedback, namely act-outcome discrepancy that truly accounts for resulting changes in behavior and affect.

Scalability of affect reward is ignored- Affect increases not because of discrepancy alone, but also because of the importance of a goal. Simply rewarding behavior with badges, likes, level upgrades etc. is a fool's errand is those tokens mean nothing, and will result in minimal engagement or boredom from the recipient no matter how surprising they are. Think for example of that underwhelming LinkedIn endorsement you just received for a skill you do not have.

Affect does not intrinsically predict long-term value- Feeling good or bad about something does not mean that you will think better about it after the feeling is gone. Many of our regrets stem from the fact that what seemed great in the moment is not so great in retrospect because we were momentarily swayed by affect, whether that affect represented a moment of lust, anger, hunger, or the mere novelty of an internet link.

Positive affect is not a pleasure- Positive affect is not a pleasure like eating a pie, it is more like an itch, a craving that energizes and spurs you to action.

Gamification is misunderstood by those who profess to understand it, and has therefore not been consciously applied to business networks, in spite of the fact that gamification is necessary to make networks work. The influence of gamification in networks is incidental or accidental, and is attributed to aspects of behavior that seem hardly game like in nature. For example, surprising compliments or encouragement for sales behavior provides the same spark to behavior that a 'badge' would, but it is rarely attributed to gamification principles. In other words, you don't need to explain rules in order to apply rules, and as we will see, explanation reveals the gamification principles that underscore not just business networks, but the networks that make all of our social institutions work.

Gamified Business Networks

Motivation depends upon demand, or the extrinsic events that are contingent upon the form or frequency of behavior. Feedback is the measure of our progress while performing a task, and as we have demonstrated, becomes motivational when it is unexpected and positive, and is non-motivational when it is expected and when it is unexpected and negative. To understand and systematically apply timing principles to raise incentives to cohere to and future goals is called gamification, and is implicitly used to enable and empower behavior and its estimable goals. Gamification is the unmentioned but critical aspect behind many of the networking rules proposed in the first part of this book.

For example, to gamify a private network, new diverse and unexpected feedback from different sources, including, joint calls, leads, one to one meetings, and referrals is provided and recorded. To gamify a sales network, different aspects of a salesperson's performance are also isolated, rewarded, and recorded. Smaller rewards that are unexpectedly scattered about a person's day are better than large rewards that are the expected consequence of a couple weeks' work (e.g. a paycheck). These networking rules motivate behavior because they implicitly elicit the positive affect or 'feelings' that drive behavior. As the saying goes, no man is an island, but no network is either, and how one will be motivated in a private network for sales is dependent upon other social networks that affect our lives. From the political and religious to the personal and familial, we live in web of networks, and to understand them is to impart the ability to predict and control our futures. As I will argue next, the wellspring of genius, productivity, and happiness does not come from inspiration, heredity, or even the water, but our innate curiosity nourished and directed by the networks we live in.

Chapter 8

A Networked World

The Networks around us

This book has emphasized the psychology of business networks, but networks are all around us. Social and business networks are interconnected, and the incentive structures that they impose are subtle, often non-conscious and misunderstood, and result in behavior in conformance or contrary to the purpose of the network itself.

We use the term network rather than social group because 'to network' underscores the dynamics of interaction between people and how those interactions and the consequences of those actions motivate behavior. Networks simply are the social scaffolding that allow humans to trade goods and services through the token economies of personal regard and money. They are the framework for incentive. Arrange and time them just so, and we can create communities of good will, contentment, and genius. Ignore or misunderstand them, and we create dysfunctional economies that lead to unhappiness, discontent, and ignorance. As we have seen, incentives are malleable things, and can be high or low depending upon our sense and understanding of timing.

Network Gamification

A network is a collection of multiple concurrent contingencies or demands that induce the trade of information between members. Our three individuals in a farmer's market are networked because they demand information from each other. However, the importance of each of their demands are inextricably tied to other social networks that have their own unique demands. Bob, Tom, and Danielle may have other mouths to feed, and must keep the respect of family and friends by being successful in their trade, and through the display of their material success, look the part.

Networks are often interconnected to other networks, and we are confronted with a host of demands that reflect not our business networks, but our social networks as well. These networks reflect the institutions of society, from educational to religious to political networks that that all want something from us. We constantly have to juggle these demands, and if they are incoherent, we have conflicts, but if coherent, they can mutually reinforce each other and make us paragons of motivation.

When we examine networks, our perspective is limited to the task at hand, and when we manipulate or gamify them, we are generally focused on altering performance feedback on the immediate task. That is a mistake, as behavior on an immediate task is often motivated by the indeterminate feedback from many other networks. This brings us to a definition of two types of gamification:

Task gamification is maximizing the variability of performance feedback within a task.

Network gamification is maximizing the variability of performance feedback between tasks.

To understand task gamification is to understand the source of motivation of someone who plays a game of solitaire. The variances in the task are derived from the task itself, and the importance of the task is determined by those variances and an expected reward (e.g., a prize for completing a solitaire game). Network gamification is different. It involves distinct interconnected tasks and their respective rewards, and can as we will see involve the fate of civilizations, or the game of Civilization.

Let's say that you are Julius Caesar, newly embarking on a career of conquest and empire building. You are the nexus of all decisions for your budding civilization, and you need to make sure that your citizens are happy, that you are always conquering new territories and gaining rich resources, and that you have an eye out for political intrigue and the advances of your neighbors who also have empires to build. These are all unpredictable tasks in themselves, but when interconnected and taken as a whole, are enough to keep you preoccupied, alert, and not a little stressed. Unless of course you can take a time out from your exploits to go to the bathroom, or can set the difficulty level for your efforts to normal or easy.

Building a civilization is a lot like 'Civilization' type games, whose addictive charms derived from the mundane tasks of setting taxes, building roads, developing new technologies, providing entertainment for the masses, and raising and directing armies. The multiplicity of interlocking parallel tasks under uncertainty can be an entertaining and addictive thing if timed just right, and luckily, '4X' games (short for explore, expand, exploit, and exterminate) are up to the challenge. Because the timing of the challenges can be set by the player to maximize interest, an individual can be merrily focused on being a legend in his own mind while not minding his own career, relationships, or education that are not similarly adjustable.

Caesar Gamified

Games can be supremely addictive because we can easily set the feedback parameters. You can set settings from hard to easy, and if you have a human opponent, choose one whose skills equally match yours. You in other words manage the feedback timing of the demands the game produces, and therefore can maximize your engagement and satisfaction. The question is, can we takes the lessons of gamification and apply them to our business and social institutions? The answer is yes, and have done so in the past, but have yet to recognize it. Consider the following historical '4X' game, played in real time by real persons on the hard setting. The players had only one life to live, and resurrection was not in the cards. To survive, they had to be schooled in the rules, and since there were none, they had to make them up. They had to learn to survive very quickly, because everyone was demanding something from them now. It may be said that it was the best educational environment that ever was, for those who could survive it that is. It was the quintessential school of hard knocks, and in the judgment of history, the best there ever was.

The School of Hard Knocks

"In Italy, for thirty years under the Borgias, they had warfare, terror, murder and bloodshed, but they produced Michelangelo, Leonardo da Vinci and the Renaissance. In Switzerland, they had brotherly love and five hundred years of democracy and peace – and what did that produce? The cuckoo clock." Orson Welles in the movie 'The Third Man'

It is commonly believed that educational environments should be nice, comforting, and hermetically sealed environments that process your children like delicate sausages, with the resulting product fully acculturated in the ways of a demanding world. That hasn't worked so well for most children, so how does an educational network process them for best results? For the best sausages that posterity has produced, it's best not to see how they are made, unless you are in the business of making great sausages. For processing people in the ways of the world, the analogy is the same. Consider a social network that arguably produced some of the best-educated people ever who went beyond the mere acquisition to the production of excellent knowledge that stood the test of time. Not a pretty sight to see since the society was wasteful and discarded many who could have learned and contributed, but for those few who were its beneficiaries, boy did it work!

It was the worst of all possible worlds, but in the eyes of posterity the best. Certainly, no educator would have recommended this place, let alone prophesize for it great or even mediocre prospects. It was a city and a state without power or light, with no modern medicine, conveniences or machines, and with fewer gifts than any society on our planet today. It was a place where the average life span was 40 years, where half the population was treated like slaves and most likely were slaves. Women's rights were nonexistent, and warfare was a constant and favored feature. Indeed, it was a miracle that it survived. Yet it belied all expectations, and became the shining star of western civilization, the fountainhead of science, art, philosophy, and politics, and the inspiration and wellspring for Western culture for the more than two thousand years to follow.

Athenian culture, and the culture of classical Greece, derived from a network of city-states that were jealous of their perquisites, stature, and knowledge. It was a competitive arrangement to say the least, fail and you're dead. Aware of their precarious state, they were anxious to master an unforgiving world because they had the opportunity and encouragement *to* master it. What created the obsessive desire to learn and explain new things? It wasn't just the fact that there was a mystery laying 'out there', it was the fact that inquisitiveness was rewarded by every aspect of society. Competition was fever pitch, and came from everywhere. The great minds of the time were created in such a cauldron of incentive. Thus, Socrates was possible and recognized his possibilities because Socrates, despite his cantankerousness, was wanted. Classical Greek society (with the exception of Sparta) with all its randomness and chaos was heavily gamified. But how do we transfer the record of a civilization's success to a local one? It's as simple as understanding why we play and watch a game of football.

All Football is Local

So here's the game plan I propose: Let's cut the middlemen and start drafting fictional, computer-simulated leagues. Let's begin with the cities that don't have much in the way of sports to get a foothold. Let's create fake players with richly detailed statistics, let's simulate complete seasons, and let's sell some schwag. Let's make this alternate reality real. This is no crazier than, say, paying grown men to play outside in a freezing field. Go Klondike Bars! –Samuel Arbesman

In the year 2045, football was purchased for a zillion dollars by Disney. Following up on its successful purchase of Pixar, Star Wars, the World Wrestling Federation, and the Catholic Church, Disney took the sport and gave it its own spin. Using the latest technology, all high school, college and pro games were rendered down to the last spectator and blade of grass. The games had action, suspense, competition, and movie stars! Naturally, the games were a lot cheaper to produce than the earlier homespun variety, which withered given the competing interest of this much better produced form of entertainment. So local athletes lost the incentive to play, and the sport devolved into little stadiums, scarce attendance, and poor play. This example of course is absurd, for football will always remain local, or will it?

In the future, Burt will be our starting quarterback, forever.

Football is an example of a gamified social network that provides multiple incentives from many different sources for improving the simple abilities of throwing, catching, tackling, dodging, running, and kicking. As standalone activities, they are hardly interesting in themselves, and left to ourselves we would likely prefer to 'stand alone'. Of course, as a game, we can participate well enough with just the interest of a few peers to keep our interest high. However, to raise interest to obsession is to court excellence, and perhaps effort worthy of a hall of fame. So how you do this? A lot of incentives mainly, occurring all the time and from all over the place. So what are the diverse goals that drive the humdrum kid into the driven athlete who will stop at nothing to earn his success?

Consider John, a budding NFL superstar who being in grade school, has a lot to look forward to. Motivation is one of them, which thankfully comes in many guises and times. John is looking forward to the many rewards, some present and some in the future that his excellence on the field will bring. Of course, with those rewards come demands as the NFL to a girlfriend must meet their own expectations as well. Thus, he must:

Play football well to *be drafted into the NFL*

Play football well to *receive a college scholarship*

Play football well to *gain the support of the crowd*

Play football well to *receive the praise of teammates and coaches*

Play football well to *impress a pretty girl.*

Play football well to *enjoy the thrill of the game.*

These demands confer different rewards that are timed differently. Entertaining the prospect of these rewards both present and future for playing football energizes the player to focus and to be obsessed with maximizing his football skills. That end is what we find among even members of the lowest strata of society, who are motivated to achieve excellence because the network makes it so. Finally, excellence can include creativity as well, and here again it is a gamified network that is the medium that incubates, promotes, and inspires genius.

All Shakespeare is Local

We should be thankful that Hollywood cannot emulate football, yet. But Hollywood certainly can emulate mass entertainment, and move it from a locally produced affair to something generated in Hollywood by throngs of technicians, producers, actors, and marketers who produce amusements as finely crafted, complex, and expensive as a Boeing 777. We know locally produced entertainment from school plays to the Little Theater, but there is little to recommend them save a mother's love for the actors, mainly kinfolk who lure you away from your DVR to see shows that you would normally not even cancel a dental appointment to see. Although giving up football to Hollywood is sacrilege, giving up on our initiative to produce our own entertainment has vanished, and we are not in the least concerned. After all, truly great stuff can only be made in Hollywood, which brings up the following question. Can we come up with great stuff locally? For the supreme example of an affirmative answer to this question, consider that all it takes is a village, or in this case, the city of London, which in 1585 was in contemporary standards just a medium sized town of 180,000 souls, or about the same population of contemporary Jackson, Mississippi. It was Shakespeare's London that the stage flourished, and the pens of Marlow, Johnson, and Shakespeare and countless other playwrights were lauded and admired. Was the play the thing, or was the audience or audiences the key to their inspiration and motivation to write?

The question arises, how did our ancestors get motivated in the past when feedback for what you did was sparse and located in proverbial haystacks, or for that matter, in the hands of proverbial hayseeds? More to the point, how did they get motivated not only to create, but to continually improve their creation? As the next example provides, it came from a ready and varied audience that gave you that information quickly and from myriad different sources: from the rafters to the streets and from the bedroom, and with a shout, a proclamation, and a lovers glance. That's the movie 'Shakespeare in Love' for you, wherein our hero found motivation and inspiration from those who would listen and had an ear for a good listen, which happened at that time to be everybody. The movie rings true not just for Shakespeare, but for his peers. In Elizabethan England, the audience didn't read much, but they certainly wanted to listen, and a good reason to listen is what preachers, and politicians, and above all, playwrights provided them to listen to. In London at this time the play *was* the thing, and for all classes, ages, and sexes, the theater was *the* social media in those days, a place to congregate, mingle, ogle, pass the time, and be informed and entertained. As the historian Daniel Boorstin recounts *"In two weeks during the 1596 season a Londoner could have seen eleven performances of ten different plays at one playhouse, and on no day would he have had to see a repeat performance of the day before........Playwriting had quickly become a growth industry and a profession. Of the twelve hundred plays offered in London theaters in the half century after 1590, some nine hundred were the work of about fifty professional playwrights."*[7]

The great popularity of the theater translated into the rich and demanding feedback for theatrical accomplishment, and it came from all sides, as the poet's voice, whether written down or just shouted down was quickly corrected by a host of real and imagined sources represented by wife, family, peers and posterity who had an ear for the spoken word and a mind to remark upon it. This diverse feedback motivated and honed the skills of a host of playwrights who labored unceasingly to get their just desserts, and as with any good dessert, the crème always rises to the top. Enter Shakespeare.

Shakespeare had no choice but to be creative because he had to simultaneously meet multiple disparate standards for approval. Things like this:

Write a great play and *be immortalized by posterity*

Make the play cheap to produce and *satisfy your financial backers*

Include sex and violence and *gain the favor of the audience*

Have good roles for your actors and *gain the praise of your cast and director.*

Have pratfalls and jokes and *gain the favor of the queen.*

Have romance and odes to love and *seduce your paramour.*

Because of the rich feedback environment provide by the social networks of Elizabethan England, Shakespeare was motivated to not only create but to hone his creation to literary perfection to match the variants in demand that satisfied all of them. In his case, the feedback worked, but it was an entire ecosystem of networked incentives that made Shakespeare be. So, in this day and age, how can you remake these heady times and their brilliant accomplishment and inspiration? Ultimately, it must start with knowledge of how networks work. Unfortunately, this knowledge is fragmentary and poorly applied, resulting in broken networks that may elicit behavior opposite of what they are intended to create.

Broken Networks

The fundamental problem is that the gap in educational achievement, which is a key in our technological economy, is due in my opinion -- and the opinion of many, including Arne Duncan, our secretary of education -- to the fact that the families of the poor who are not very educated are not talking to their children, interacting with their children, insisting they do their homework and so on. Should we say it's a failure? Let's say it's an error of omission.- Jerome Kagan

In part one of this book, I demonstrated how dysfunctional networks in business occur because networks are inadvertently designed to *be* dysfunctional. This results in unintended consequences for events that should have been wholly predictable. The networks that embody our major social institutions are no different, and despite the best of intentions create unexpected consequences because of our misunderstanding of how networks and human motivation work.

In economics, a free and unfettered market means that all people in all places can compete for the same business, and the competitive market place will hone the skills of those who wish to compete, and drive out those who cannot. This means that we can trade and network with anyone, and get our goods and services from anywhere, including the human assets that make economies tick. By importing gifted and well-educated people from abroad, economies become more competitive, but this comes at the cost of ignoring the development of our own homegrown human assets. The solution ironically comes from those very people we seek to import, namely the social networks that made their accomplishment possible. Importing gifted people from abroad means you are not only importing their skills, but also the social networks that create and sustain those skills. We import in other words not only gifted people, but their parenting skills. Do we understand this lesson? Apparently not.

The answer to global competition is to upgrade the engineering, manufacturing, distribution, and marketing of products and services. The cost of this can be immense with long lead times and uncertain results, and is deferred to the uncertain whims of government. However, to upgrade your human resources, you need but upgrade your social networks, which cost very little and can be performed on the fly. For example, to upgrade your sales force, a sales manager must look first to designing the business networks that support and encourage the sales effort. Similarly, to improve educational systems, they must be gamified to include not just changing the variability of feedback of the task, but also of the larger ramifications of completing that task, from the approval of a parent to a classmate to the admissions officer of a college. That requires expanding gamification from the task alone to social networks comprised of multiple individuals who demand and reward learning accomplishment.

An example of this is the online mathematics tutorial called the Khan Academy. The Khan Academy is the supreme example of task gamification in an educational setting. With self paced lessons, badges, rewards, certificates, and prompt feedback that guides individual students to the correct answer, the Khan Academy motivates students to eagerly attend and learn. However, although the site adjusts the timing of rewards to increase the momentary utility or importance of paying attention to the task, it does not and cannot change the degree of rewards for accomplishment. To do that requires a human element, namely a person or persons within a social network who demand and reward performance.

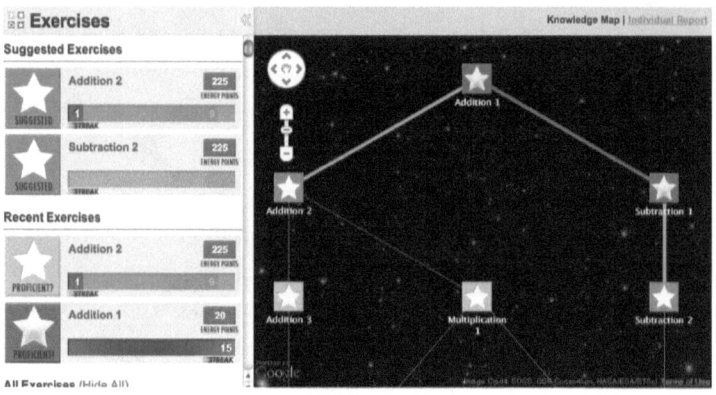

The Math of 'Khan'

When teachers, parents, peers and society reward performance, as in classical Greece, performance will follow. The key is not the enrichment of the physical environment; after all, ancient Greece and Shakespearean London were by all modern standards impoverished, but rather it must come from the intelligent provision of demand. Demand in turn can be arranged easily, quickly, and for next to nothing. Nonetheless, as with business networks, performance still must have its metrics, and the rubber must still hit the road. For education, that means learning a marketable skill, but for academics, it means teaching one, and that again demonstrates how networks can set us unintentionally off the road and right into a tree.

Academic Networks

"When I read academic literature, all too often by paragraph three I'm lost in a morass of quantitative analysis that is far beyond not only my abilities but those of almost every business person I've ever met. In my view, the authors devote far too much of their time conducting research and writing about it in articles that only their peers understand and too little time actually teaching. As a result, their students are getting progressively less for their money, a guarantee of future serious trouble for higher education…

… A couple of years ago, a valued faculty member who was responsible for a prolific output of financial research at a well-known business school resigned. This caused great distress within the college, as the administration feared that the school's rankings would suffer because it would no longer be associated with his scholarship. But while he was the school's most successful scholar, he certainly didn't teach anything related to his research. How practical was that research anyway? I've worked in the financial area for 50 years and I didn't have a clue as to what his most recent articles were about -- and nor did various business colleagues to whom I showed them. If we couldn't decipher his writings, for whom were they intended? My answer: The community of scholars who write for one another but not for their students and certainly not for business executives who are interested in practical ideas that might actually work" **Knowledge@Wharton Law and Public Policy Research Article**

Why Business Schools Teach Transparency but Practice Ambiguity

Published: February 13, 2013 in Knowledge@Wharton

Go to grade and high school, and teachers are invariably rewarded by how well they teach a settled body of knowledge. Go to college, and although you are going learn accepted knowledge, you want to learn new and unsettled knowledge. Like sitting on the foot of Socrates, you want to be at the moment of creation, except of course for Socrates himself, who would have doubted the whole enterprise. However, how can you measure the excellence of your thought when it may be theoretical, rhetorical, and just plain untestable? Educators have an answer for that. Academic accomplishment that can't be measured can at least be metered, and your published record in academic journals suffices to attest to your intellectual acumen and pending if not actual ability to move the world.

Moving the academic network to rewarding quantity over quality certainly has its benefits, if you survey the massive amount of academic business literature that is published annually, but by tying performance to a measure that has no practical meaning, nothing practical can or will come of it. Overall, like business networks, academic accomplishment works when it is tied to networks that demand practical things. For example, research in a teaching hospital is valuable because it is published, but also because it leads to valuable things like new medical procedures and vaccines. Unfortunately, academic networks for the social sciences don't work because unlike applied sciences, their findings are difficult to apply, verify, or reproduce. Because there is no incentive to derive practical knowledge, then impractical knowledge is the replacement standard, and it is gauged by the favor of your peers, not an audience that expects solutions to real problems. Thus, academics judge the merits of other academics, and devolve into the arcane language of a select circle that can understand it alone, and perhaps not even that.

With academic literature, it's the tonnage of stuff that you write that counts for status and tenure, and academics are loath to depart from it since their worth is tied to its bulk, not its practicality. Like a garage overfilling with sentimental but worthless objects, the world of academic thought is just as overstuffed, and is still for the most part, a world of glorified garbage.

Getting down to business

What if one year, in a spasm of superhuman creativity, you were to write 20,000 articles that were published in all the best academic journals? And what if no one actually reads them, let alone put their lessons to use? Welcome to the wonderful world of business pedagogy, where business journalese takes aim at the concerns of business managers, and promptly overshoots its target, or better said, shoots itself in the foot. This is the problem with academic business research, which pretty much goes unread by an audience that only has 10 seconds for you to get to the point. Since getting to your point or more specifically marketing your point is a skill that academics rarely possess, the audience moves to those white-collar types who become bestowed with street cred by earning a billion or so for General Electric, IBM, or Starbucks. It's sort of like Dr. Phil becoming a genius psychologist because he 'cured' a million of so poor souls on Oprah. In an article on the state of business journalese 'The Economist'[8], the global accrediting agency for business schools recommended that the value of research for the research faculty should be judged not by listing their citations in journals, but by demonstrating their impact on the workaday world. Since journal articles don't have much of an impact, you can get the drift. Ultimately it is not the recommendations of academic research that count in the real world, but how easily they can be generated by clear, succinct, and most importantly, useful explanations. For business people, usefulness is measured in how explanations can translate into procedures that provide an edge in the Darwinian marketplace. Hence, nonsense has the shelf life of a Care Bear in the Cretaceous. Too bad there is no global accrediting agency for the social sciences as there is for business. It would be good indeed for those of us interested in the business of living.

Lack of incentives make children value education less and the perversity of incentives make educators create less valuable knowledge. In the old Soviet Union, a proverb among workers was that I pretend to work and you pretend to pay me. Similarly, if I pretend to learn and you pretend to teach me something of practical value (particularly in college) two dysfunctional networks interlock, making education even more dysfunctional.

Because of the perverse nature of academic networks, the social sciences have become a balkanized mess of conflicting ideologies and findings, leaving us to the mercies of the pop psychologists, pundits, and journalists who without sound explanations of behavior at the ready will make up their own. This results in cockeyed interpretations of the business network that as we will note would not even make a pilgrim proud.

Chapter 9

Conventional Wisdom

What is Networking?

The wisdom and insight offered so far in this book are unconventional to say the least. Citing obscure economic and neurological facts is hard to digest when compared to the comfortable truisms and happy talk of the world of self-help. So now it's time to counter those new ideas with some good old fashioned ones, which speak of conventions about human behavior that have been trusted for hundreds of years. If traditional wisdom is to be believed, our minds are beset by a tumultuous sea of inner motivators, urges, instincts, drives, and feelings that are named differently, are mixed up in countless permutations, and are dutifully served up by academic and self-help pundits alike to illuminate in metaphors of how our minds work. Likewise, it takes one metaphorical process to know one, or in the case of self-help, to control one. Thus, we summon our inner power, higher consciousness, sense of optimism, or need to achieve to overcome the urges, negative thoughts, and bad vibes that set us down the wrong path in life.

In this book, I have dispensed with such things by describing motivation and in particular, the motivation to trade information to be dependent upon its extrinsic properties alone, and attributing intrinsic motivators, or the 'energy' that makes us go to how that information is arranged, timed, and measured. This is akin to attributing the arousal of one's appetite at the dinner table by not just the prospect of a delicious meal, but also in large measure to how deftly the table setting is arranged. Plain and simple, motivation is caused by extrinsic motivators and how the likelihood of attaining them unexpectedly changes from moment to moment, and that we are a slave to our circumstances, not our wills.

Nonetheless, 'them's fightin' words' for psychologists. Motivation simply has to be a lot more complex than that, and conventional wisdom makes it so by hypothesizing a numberless array of needs, drives, and impulses that fall under the rubric of 'intrinsic motivation'. Intrinsic motivation is why we network: a need for affiliation, a sense of equity or a feeling of friendship, all distilled into the motto of 'givers gain'. It is not so much the obligation but the pleasure of giving that makes business networks successful.

This brings us to the consideration of the popular literature of business networking, a diversity of work that proves to be rather un-diverse in its uniform definition of what business networking is. Derived primarily from popular motivational literature, networking is in a word the art of ingratiation.

What is Networking?

Here are some definitions of business networking from the most popular writers on networking.

Devora Zack – *"networking is the art of building and maintaining connections for shared positive outcomes."*

Michael Goldberg – *"Networking is simply a proactive approach to meeting people with a view towards learning something and potentially helping others."*

Ivan Misner – *"Networking is the process of developing contacts and relationships, enhance your knowledge, expand your sphere of influence, or serve the community."*

"Networking is about forming and nurturing mutually beneficial relationships, which bring you new connections with large numbers of people who can help your business in other ways."

In this collective perspective, networking is about relationships rather than transactions, emotional rather than logical values, sociological rather than economic causes, behavior that is intrinsically rather than extrinsically caused, and is selfless rather than selfish. It is as if economics stops at the door when we stop trading things for money, or more succinctly, when simple extrinsic incentives are shown the door in favor of intrinsic incentives that are easy to confound you with. Above all, underscoring these definitions is the belief that individuals are inherently good, and will in the end do the right thing by paying back your personal investment in them. Like Harry Bailey's friends coming to his aid when his Business and Loan fails, the friends of such a loyal networker will not forget him. It's a wonderful life is it not?

Well, no.

The problem is conflating business values with social values. The individuals in your business network are not your relatives; they participate for economic and not personal reasons. Business networking is more like running a lemonade stand than having a family reunion. One does not run a lemonade stand to build connections, meet people, help or share with others, or enhance your knowledge. You open a lemonade stand because you *contractually* exchange value for value, and you do the same when you participate in a business network.

Defining business networking as a social process that incidentally builds business rather than an economic process that expressly builds business makes the rules of networking, tentative, unclear, and ultimately counterproductive to sales. Effective business networking means something else, with rules and feedback that are clear and prompt, and value that is logical and predictable. As we shall see from our overview of the popular literature on networking, playing nice will not get you the business, or the girl.

The Popular Networking Literature

Elevator Pitch: The art of making a quick sales pitch to someone who is in an elevator with you. For true sales pros, the elevator pitch is much shorter, as when you are pitching the value of your worthless life to God as you are falling down an elevator shaft.

Compared to the near limitless number of popular books on selling, business networking books are far fewer, and are a drop in the literary bucket. The main reason perhaps for this is that networking is generally viewed as an indirect way of making sales. Its main attribute is the art of ingratiation, not salesmanship. In other words, networking is a relatively brainless affair, where you impress people with your earnestness, selflessness, and ability to describe your terrific product in a great one-minute elevator pitch that they will promptly engrave in their memory and regurgitate promptly when in front of potential referrals. Of course, because you are such a nice and virtuous person, they know that they will someday get something from you in return.

Fat chance!

Because networking at root requires a leap of faith that too often ends you at the bottom of the canyon rather than on the other side. But if hope springs eternal from the salesperson's breast, then this type of networking is right for you. But does it work? Well, ask Miles.

John trying out his elevator pitch with Priscilla

Networking books uniformly follow what I would call the Miles Standish sales approach, where you don't set the stage for your grand sales call, but your friends do. If you recall your grade school history lesson, Miles Standish and John Alden were two friends who were vying for the hand of Priscilla Collins, the only eligible English girl within three thousand miles. Too shy, uncertain, and bumbling to make a proposal himself, Miles asked John to make the proposal for him. John dutifully made the proposal for Miles, but Priscilla interjected, "speak for yourself John", and John proposed and married Priscilla.

Translated into the network jargon of the pop network literature, Miles met Alden at a Plymouth Rock networking meeting, and using the givers gain motto, convinced John to make the referral for him for his close contact Priscilla. Forgetting the networking mantra of selflessness, and discarding Miles' elevator pitch, John closed the sale for himself, and lived happily ever after.

The point is, no one is going to network for you unless they are sure of getting something in return. John was not sure of what he would get from Miles, and grabbed the sure thing, namely Priscilla, rather than follow Miles' instructions. Don't get me wrong, kindness is a splendid human trait, but so is earning a living, and very often reality has to intrude upon the sunnier aspirations of the race. Where reality does not intrude are those popular writers on the business networking, who deliver the networking experience to you, sunny side up.

Devora Zack

In her book 'Networking for people who hate networking', Devora Zack makes networking success all about you. This book treats us to a flurry of mentalisms, but little insight. We learn a lot of pop psychology fluff about why introverts differ from extraverts, about mental flexibility and mental agility, and of course how a right attitude fortified by a few tablespoons of will power makes the networking world go round.

The book is full of full of common sense tactics that we all know, like stressing to a fellow in a job interview to keep his hair combed and tie on straight. Thus, at a networking meeting, to get the best results you volunteer to help, arrive early, get in a food line to better socialize with your peers, etc. More a self-help than a business book, it ultimately fails at both.

Michael Goldberg

The tip off to Goldberg's networking gambit is that he is all about helping others, for a fee of course. Even saints must eat you know. The problem is that Goldberg obviously wants to preach his gospel in an unsaintly fashion, and comes across more like P.T Barnum than St. Francis. From his web site, it is obvious that he wants to sell you something far more than teach you something. With a full product line of cds, workbooks, and Michael himself, who will kindly fly down for a small fee so speak to your group, networking is not just a simple skill, it is an industry! So what is Michael's special wisdom? It's nothing new. From his book 'Knock Out Networking', he imparts advice that even the bashful Miles Standish doubtless heard before.

"Few people engage in networking, and even fewer are good at it. Why do people avoid this low-cost proven means of making exponential gains in their personal and professional lives? Funny you ask! It's mainly because of fear! Some people shy away from networking because they think it involves selling or politicking, but those activities run contrary to the positive relationship-building aspect of networking. Others simply don't know what to do and are intimidated by meeting people in person. The myriad fears associated with networking can be defused simply by knowing the "rules to networking" or, what I refer to in Chapter 2, as "The Pool Rules of Networking."

The pool rules of networking allude to the rules that you must follow to make a public swimming pool fun and friendly for all. Make sure your swimsuit fits, do not dive in the shallow end, shower before entering, swim when a lifeguard is around, no horseplay, etc. Goldberg's pool rules are similar, and just as obvious. So just be nice, pithy (use your elevator pitch), unselfish (learn all about the other person), look good (dress well and comb your hair), never 'sell' (let them sell to you first), and be professional (whatever that means).

These rules pertain to individual behavior within a network meeting, not the 'pool rules' that the network organizers should follow, and are the rules that really count. For the managers of a public swimming pool these rules are a clean and safe venue, lifeguards and lifesaving equipment available, availability of chairs and tables to sit down and lounge, and a nice concession stand. Unfortunately, Goldberg doesn't outline the pool rules for those who run business networks, and blames our emotional reaction to a poorly run network to our irrational fear. This of course is nonsense. Poorly designed networks elicit fear, and well-designed networks mitigate it. Well run networking meetings also reduce many of the other bad emotions people experience when they arrive at meeting that is poorly designed, like boredom, frustration, regret, and depression. It is because of etiquette and not a personality deficit that we are fearful or suffer other bad emotions when at a poorly run networking meeting. We don't want to speak up and complain about the lack of introductions, poor food, bad venue, and uninteresting crowd, and therefore simmer in the stew of bad emotions that follow. So according to Goldberg, what is networking really about?

"Networking is simply a proactive approach to meeting people with a view towards learning something and potentially helping others. The process involves face-to-face interaction! Being active on social-media sites can facilitate networking, but there is so much more to it than that. Networking is about learning from and potentially helping people. That's it! Networking is NOT about selling a product or service or handing out resumes. If you learn from and potentially help the right people, they tend to help you right back! The essence of networking is knowing what you want (more business, land a job, learn something, solve a problem, social reasons), going to the right places(associations, chambers of commerce, conferences, networking groups, alumni organizations, social clubs), saying the right things (strong intro, asking good questions, delivering an elevator pitch, exchanging business cards, creating interest and engagement), meeting the right people (those that can help you accomplish your goal – economic buyer, hiring manager, referral source), and following up the right way (promptly making good on promises, next steps, providing info, setting up a meeting, staying in touch, developing relationships over time, expanding a strong database, establishing an awesome reputation, offering great value).

Who should network? If you're a business owner, sales rep, recruiter, fundraiser, politician, job searcher, corporate warrior looking to advance, or looking for the love of your life, you should be networking.

My networking model is simply going to the right places, saying the right things, and meeting the right people. Of course, the right places, right things, and right people will vary depending on what you're looking for – type of job, type of business, or the man/woman of your dreams. But the model remains the same —who, what, where.

The benefit of networking is establishing long-term relationships over time so you always have resources to help you (and your network) with life's endeavors. The fun part is you get to help them right back!

According to Goldberg, network is all about ingratiation, but in the right places and with the right people. Nonetheless, as I have argued in this book, long-term relationships require a social or meeting structure to mediate them. How do you stay in touch, develop relationships, and expand your 'awesome' reputation? Is it through email, phone calls, or a lunch date? Goldberg overlooks that fact that long-term relationships take time to be valuable, and you need rules to set up the meeting venue, what is to be said, the roles of other people in your network, and above all to use your time wisely. In other words, networking needs to be efficient, and building and running an efficient network is something that Goldberg does not explain. He could learn a bit from our next author, who has built an efficient business network as efficient and uniform as the McDonald's hamburger chain, but with a value proposition that overflows with empty calories.

Ivan Misner

"Great networkers don't need to do much selling, because many people come to them, ready to buy."

Ivan Misner is one slick guy. Having founded and built the business-networking group BNI into a worldwide empire, he should be the final word on how to understand and build effective business networks. Well, forget the building part of the equation, for he has his pre-fab solution for you, his BNI network of course. To make sure you know he has the final word, he has written twelve books on networking, each more final than the next, and all lauding the supreme virtues of his networking Levittown.

Misner breaks down business networks by their most rudimentary obligations towards each other. For example, networking at Chamber of Commerce business socials comes with no obligation, and are casual contacts. Strong contacts however are epitomized (naturally) by groups that are like service clubs (e.g. the Rotary) and BNI that do require something of you. The Rotary wants you to do community service, but BNI requires you to serve up leads, which is a much better deal. Casual contacts on the other hand are groups the Chamber of Commerce and local business associations. However, because the people you meet at local chamber meetings are not obligated to serve you up with regular referrals, BNI again is a much better choice. As you can guess, all roads lead to BNI, and whether your contacts are strong or weak, networking is your problem and BNI is your cure.

Misner comes up short in discussing the dynamics of business networks, and insists on the one size fits all model for business networks. A bigger fault with Misner is that he is concerned with erecting virtual barriers to entry for his enterprise, and although he is full of advice on what do when going to BNI or other networking function, he shies away from showing you how to set up your own networking function.

Misner's simple-minded approach to networks neatly dovetails with his simple-minded BNI referral network, which nonetheless needs six officers per chapter to reinforce the equally simple-minded BNI rulebook. That is part of the plan, since if a well-run networking group needs many chiefs to go with all those paying Indians, and you will need a lot of Indians of course, you will be less inclined to try it by yourself. Overall, Misner's book follows the standard good neighbor policy of networking, where a salesperson is rewarded by folks who will recognize your goodness in the end, if you can wait that long. However, if you can wait *really* long, and contact lots more folks, networking paradise is just a thousand clicks away.

Reid Hoffman, as told to Ben Casnocha

If you founded and head up a multibillion-dollar social network, with all that money you don't need to be troubled to take the time to write a book on networking, just tell it to a scribe. I should be so lucky in my own affairs. With Misner, who at least wrote all his stuff, all networking roads lead to BNI. For the book 'The Startup of You', written with by the founder of LinkedIn as told to Ben, you know where this road is going.

This book is a commercial for LinkedIn and the philosophy of networking that its founder would like you to BuyIn. First off, Hoffman disparages the 'old school' of networking, which is dependent upon transactions, or what I can get from you. The new school of networking is about relationships, or what you can do for someone else. It's about positioning yourself in good stead with the hundreds of folks who may be of service to you in the future. This is the mantra of ingratiation writ large, where every one of your hundreds of contacts need a little loving now and then, which you obliging do once or twice a year with an endorsement, a like, or an 'inmail' asking how the wife and kids are doing. The saying goes that no good deed goes unpunished, but for Hoffman, good deeds fits into the social karma of life, with just rewards for your virtue right around the bend. For me though, getting congratulated or endorsed from people I hardly know for things I have never done is not my just reward, it's just spam.

Hoffman errs by defining transactions as one-way affair, when a transaction means an immediate exchange of value. As I have argued throughout this book, this old-fashioned way of networking works just fine, it's his own creation that is flawed. LinkedIn, and its underlying philosophy of ingratiation, means the prospective and not actual exchange of value, with your return for your investment drifting in a future nether land. Although a penny in the bank earns a return in time, a penny for your thoughts is a more dubious investment, and that's exactly what Hoffman proposes. So, staying in touch with just two hundred of your contacts will help you leverage their connections with their own professional contacts, numbering maybe in the millions. Is Hoffman right? A simple question will suffice. The comedian Jimmy Fallon remarked that to find out who your true friends are in social media, just sent out an email to them asking them to help you move. Chances are strong however that when you need your friend in your LinkedIn network, none of whom will help you move. To Hoffman, networking involves 'Habitual reciprocity that becomes coated with emotion'. In other words, networking is just one big emotional Dove Bar, and he invites us all to take a bite! Knowing that what is in this bar is most likely not ice cream but rather a very different steaming pile, this is one author who won't.

Turing's Test

In this age of social connectivity, we perpetuate delusions rather than reality, and are quite happy about it, unless we are proverbially or really need a helping hand, and that's when we find that our true friends are far fewer in number than we think. We read too much meaning into the briefest of information: a 'like', an endorsement, or a view mean something when they generally mean nothing at all. It will display intelligence maybe, but not empathy, not affection, and certainly not a heightened likelihood that they will help you out when you need them, or for that matter help you move.

And that is precisely what is missing in the virtual networks like LinkedIn or Facebook that populate our time, a sense that your contacts have an intrinsic obligation to be there for you in time of need, whether it may be job advice or simply a sales referral.

They won't be.

At least your contacts sure seem intelligent, even when they post unintelligent comments or stupid pictures or ignore you when you are in the lurch. Intelligence is however not all it is cracked up to be, since if we were truly intelligent, our ethic would be more like Machiavelli than Christ. In other words, you would be looking out a lot more for number one, mainly yourself, and realistically, that is what people do.

Sometimes being intelligent depends upon seeming to be intelligent. For mathematician and cybernetic pioneer Alan Turing, seeming was all that mattered if intelligence is considered, and our present-day media has extended this argument to assuming that having intelligent friends depends upon seeming to have them. That we buy in to the Turing Test is an understatement, as we bow to the nods of virtual friends as if moving with the tide.

The 'Turing Test' derived from the hypothesis that all we know of intelligence is how it is represented to us, and if we cannot tell the difference in a conversation between a human being and a machine, we must assume that the machine is intelligent. Intelligence does not mean it will consider it intelligent to help you out. Indeed, it's often more intelligent to leave you alone.

**Avatar for yours truly,
who will be your friend, for ten bucks.**

So how to judge that the entity at the end of the line is intelligent and humane if you can't otherwise vouch for their humanity, of just being human? In the future, it will always be intelligent and humane, but it won't be human. At least it may take notice of you and just maybe send a remote controlled car to help you move. *In our vanity, even if our only future friend is named Google, that just might do.*

Intrinsic Motivation

Extrinsic Motivation: *Motivation that comes from without, such as money, titles, honors, trophies, and a date with Mary Jane. Extrinsic motivation has been found to destroy intrinsic motivation; hence the present movement to eliminate extrinsic motivation from schools, hospitals, and government, making them the efficient dynamos full of self-motivators that we know today.*

Intrinsic Motivation: *Motivation that comes from within, as opposed to extrinsic motivation, which comes without. Humanistic psychologists stress the importance of developing intrinsic motivation early in life, so that as adults we can be self-motivated without the need to have to earn a living.*

Business networking succeeds when we are motivated to participate in them, and that is because they help us attain our professional goals. I have argued that motivation is elicited by extrinsic events simply arranged, and is dependent upon how a network is designed. That is not however how conventional opinion views the matter. In this view, motivation is an internal or intrinsic thing, and represents the inner drives and motivators that can be eternally rediscovered, repackaged and represented to you, and all for a tidy fee. Because of my reduction of motivation to rudimentary principles, what's missing in this book are all those great motivational buzzwords that I implicitly consigned to the dustbin. Gone with the long-winded are catch words such as the 'power within', the seven successful habits, needs to achieve, etc. that make our motivational motors hum. Underscoring these familiar buzzwords is a much simpler premise about how our minds work, which is simple, persuasive, and equally wrong.

It starts with the guiding metaphor of human motivation popular with academic and laypeople alike is that our motivations are modular things, evolutionary add ons that like satellite radio in a modern car give us that added and distinctive feature set that sets us apart from earlier models of autos or humans. Thus, we are possessed with neural modules for language, morality, speech, and motivation. These modules can in other words be explained from the interaction of a few basic neural functions, just as all the colors of the spectrum can be derived from various admixtures of red, green, and blue. Motivation is presumably like that, with separate modules or drives set aside to respond to external and internal needs. Encompassing them all is the concept of intrinsic motivation, a word that in this author's opinion should be expelled from the psychological lexicon.

*As defined, "**intrinsic motivation** refers to motivation that is driven by an interest or enjoyment in the task itself, and exists within the individual rather than relying on any external pressure."[9] The writer Daniel Pink puts it another way, and describes it as a literal force of human nature: "We have a biological drive. We eat when we're hungry, drink when we're thirsty, have sex to satisfy our carnal urges. We also have a second drive—we respond to rewards and punishments in our environment. But what we've forgotten—and what the science shows—is that we also have a third drive. We do things because they're interesting, because they're engaging, because they're the right things to do, because they contribute to the world. The problem is that, especially in our organizations, we stop at that second drive. We think the only reason people do productive things is to snag a carrot or avoid a stick. But that's just not true. Our third drive—our intrinsic motivation—can be even more powerful."[10]*

Intrinsic motivation in other words is a distinct mental module that powers or drives behavior, and you don't need extrinsic motivators because intrinsic motivation has enough intrinsic 'smarts' to look after your long term interest. Trust your gut feelings, and you will be fine. The internet pundit Clay Shirky agrees, and with his concept of 'cognitive surplus', he argued that the web has freed us to apply our time to other productive social endeavors that are mediated by the web.[11] In his opinion, the information age is an era that encourages us to produce and share as much as we consume. So rather than wasting time watching reruns of Gilligan's Island, we are putting our time to far better use that benefits us all. Through technology, we are thus entering a new era of participation and enlightenment.

The problem with these viewpoints is that, as I have argued in this book, affect or gut feelings are poor prognosticators of the future because they are in large measure elicited by abstract rather than functional (cause-effect) elements of the environment. So, if you are repeatedly accessing your email or social network and feel aroused or 'good' about it, the momentary value of a task itself will generally over match the value of its predicted end, namely effectively keeping up with your business contacts and friends. A second problem is that intrinsic motivation is not a separate 'drive' that is un-tethered to extrinsic events, but reflects behavior that is controlled by an abstract aspect of the extrinsic motivator that reflects the way it is arranged to follow behavior, namely how it matches or mis-matches expectations. In other words, incentive motivation is primarily initiated and guided by extrinsic events. To explain and justify this position, one must resort to a neurally informed explanation of incentive motivation[3][12] that unfortunately reveals no hidden ghostly drive within the machine. Pink's third drive has no parallel in nature, and no identifiable source within the human brain. It's completely made up. But again, it doesn't matter, because good explanations and the effective and testable procedures that they suggest resolves the issue, as they always have, and as I will argue next, always will.

---

[3] In 2007 the psychologists Frederic Kaplan and Pierre-Yves Oudeyer did just that, and attributed the intrinsic motivation of children to explore and play, or behavior performed 'for its own sake' to an expected decrease in prediction error. The authors proposed that dopaminergic activity acts a learning process signal, and that this progress signal was directly computed through a hierarchy of micro-cortical circuits.

And now a word for all you dummies!

For any problem that calls out for a cure, the cure is at hand, lots of them in fact. Helpful hints and useful procedures can rain down on us like confetti, but does one have time to follow them all, let alone remember them? That's the conundrum of the 'XYZ for Dummies' book series, which embellishes and records every nugget of wisdom for every topic under the sun, from Acne to Z Systems, all for dummies of course. The 'Business Networking for Dummies' book is no exception to the formula, which outlines in Cliff Notes fashion all the separate suggestions, ideas, helpful hints, and bullet points one could ever need that could lead to networking success. However, one thing is missing in this recipe: a suitable explanation. There are 1001 ways to treat a cold, but we zero down on merely a few because we know how colds work. There are likewise 1001 ways to network to increase sales, but if we don't know how networks work, then we are hard put to choose the best, and to maximize the effectiveness of the one's we choose. The result is that we waste time, a resource a business person can least afford. So, if joining the Rotary, the Chamber, a social media site, or a for profit networking group are all equally valuable, and if there are many different approaches within them to cultivate business, then we are ultimately cast back on our own devices, and learn the hard way which networking strategies and tactics are best for us. Serves you right, dummy!

By removing networking from the muddle abstraction of relationship building to cold economics, the ends and means of networking are distilled into their psychological rudiments. This is necessary not only to succeed in business, but as we shall see, also in life.

Chapter 10

The Future of Networking

Muddles and Muggles

All human enterprises profit from proper explanations of the world. Knowing how something works gives you the knowledge to make it work, and make it work better. Unfortunately, humans don't know how motivation works, and therefore don't know how to make themselves work, and work better. This extends beyond productive labor, but to all the things that make us human, from our family and friends to the deeds and accomplishments that are the stuff of memory and anticipation. The future of networking depends upon good explanations for why we do the things we do, and it must start with a proper explanation of incentive.

Incentive

Psychology: The science of mind that may or may not involve science or mind, may or may not involve behavior, may or may not be theoretical, empirical, ethological, or logical, and may or may not be simplistic, incomprehensible, or downright obvious. Psychology, by being all definitions for all people, is an all-encompassing discipline that gives us clues to our behavior and keeps us clueless about behavior at the same time.

Incentive: The metaphorical, symbolic, or real events either present or future, real or virtual, that strengthen, alter, or otherwise change behavior. An incentive can be many things. It can be an object as large as a house, or objectified in a subtle change of feeling. It can be inferred from a change in observable behavior, or a change in the likelihood of behavior yet to come. It can be an event that 'pulls' behavior from us, like a Pavlovian reflex; it can be an event that 'pushs' and is glued to behavior like a Skinnerian positive 'reinforcer'; or it can be a mere wisp of a thought evidenced in a simple change of mind. In short, like the Cheshire cat, it is here, but never here, a tease perhaps that's needed to get us about in Neverland. It is something everyone knows and no one knows. Indeed, if this author knew for sure, he would write it here, and find the revelation no doubt very incentivizing indeed.

To understand business and social networking, our arguments stem from two simple premises:

1) People behave because they have the incentive to behave.

2) Incentives are not what you think they are.

Network interactions are guided by the mutual exchange of virtual or real objects of value or utility. However, the present utility of a behavior may not conform with its future or predicted utility due to how effectively incentives may be timed or predicted. In other words, behavior is dependent not just upon expected incentives, but how well they are arranged to be *unexpected*. This is hardly logical, but is eminently bio-logical, and reflects the fact that evolution in its wisdom didn't bestow us with new mental equipment to ramp up our motivational wits to match our newer and bigger brains, it just used old mental parts and pieces to get the motivational job done. Human motivation is a kludge because the human brain uses more primitive instincts to make motivation work with its newer thinking parts, sort of like using bailing wire, duct tape and chewing gum to enlist old parts to do new things in lieu of using a brand-new part. It all works in strange, awful, and wonderful ways, but it works.

This is a big come down from the glorious picture handed down to us by our theologians, philosophers, and psychologists that humans are somewhat special, and possess traits specially bestowed by God or nature to set us apart from our mammalian cousins. The comeuppance to this come down is the fact that humans want explanations, and won't settle for less.

The last bastion of resistance to explanation is the social sciences. The expert opinions of social scientists give us rules, but not rules of thumb, correlations, but not explanations. For us laypeople, so dependent upon who we ask or who we quote, we end up conflicted by the fog of expert opinion, and our actions become uncertain and too often, ineffectual. Expertise can be a very easy or a very hard thing, it just depends upon the quality of the explanations that you use. Have a good explanation, as in knowledge of the origins of disease, and you can become an 'expert' in a jiffy to those who those who haven't a clue, and generate with ease a score of procedures that ensure and prolong your health. On the other hand, have a bad or incomplete explanation, and your prescriptions will be unreliable, inefficient, or just plain wrong, and expertise is lost to a new class of 'experts' who purport to know better, and are incented by their privileged status to keep it that way.

In ancient times, explanations belonged only to a few, and we needed a priestly class to explain things for us. However, incumbent upon progress are better and better explanations that democratize the availability of expertise, as everyone now can predict when the sun will rise. With better explanations comes the diminishment of expertise, as we all know what to do and how to do it. But what happens if you have no time even for explanations? Then you just muddle along and end up in places you may least expect, and for the information revolution, discover that even cornucopias can soon grow stale.

Why Explanations are Important

Science Quiz: circa 1840

You live in the Florida panhandle town of Apalachicola, which is surrounded by a swamp. You can catch malaria if you are not careful. What should you do to eliminate the risk?

1) Move to Montana

2) Drain the swamp

3) Live in an airtight air-conditioned house

4) Put garlic in your shoes (an actual remedy at the time, since the garlic vapors it was thought would travel up your body to do some real good, but not of the aroma kind)

5) Shoot Cannons

Any of the first three options of course are correct, and 100% correlate with the avoidance of malaria. The other two somewhat correlate with avoiding malaria if you play your sample sizes and types right. Now fast forward to 1940, and you have the same options, plus one more. That option is to spray for mosquitoes. Why would this answer today be a no brainer? It is because you can explain malaria. You can in other words describe malaria by using metaphors from the macroscopic (epidemiology) to the microscopic (microbiology). With a few words, you can describe its origin and transmission, and from simple explanation you can derive myriad additional procedures to eliminate it from malarial vaccines to mosquito nets to yes, moving to Montana and draining the swamp. You can also quickly discount spurious remedies (garlic is out!) that may correlate with malarial relief, but explain nothing. Even more impressive is that there is no need to memorize a full list of malarial remedies, since they are easily extrapolated from a simple explanation. But what is an explanation?

Explanations are different integrated metaphorical ways of describing the same thing that are continually validated by repeated observations. Each point of view informs and corrects the other, so if you example a microbiological description of disease informs how you wash your hands and when you could of should not drink the water. Conversely, if you did drink the wrong water and did not get sick you would need to recalibrate your germ theory of disease to figure out why.

Successful science is validated by the applied sciences that get us somewhere, from jet planes to vaccines. These objects are ultimately possible because science must first explain. Because science demands multiple levels of description that must cohere, this invites a lot more room for doubt, and later, correction. In 1840, there was no biological description for malaria, which if it then existed would immediately cohere or be incoherent with common descriptions of malaria such as swamp gas, evil spirits, etc.

Multiple ways of looking at things from multiple levels results invariably in better ways of doing things. If you have a disease, or are building a business, then explanation is your best friend. Knowing why shows you infinite ways of knowing how. Thus, knowing a bit of biology or physics enables the know how to ensure health and build a technological world. Similarly, being challenged to revise one's explanation teaches a person something important that he does not know, and that is the essential part of making the salesperson and his services valuable.

A company has to motivate people to sell stuff, and up to now, there has been no need for explanation. Just give a salesperson a salary, a commission, and a quota, and their motivation will be raised sufficiently so they are focused on calling on clients and make sales. However, explain to them what incentive is and how it works, and they will be able them to perceive how it is subtly woven into the social networks that bind them. Their sales performance will improve even further because best practices are tied to best explanations, and sales teams will be able to derive better procedures from explanation to do their jobs more effectively.

The Main Incentive

Freakonomics: *The study of economics based upon the principle of incentives. Pretty freaky stuff, since it leaves out free will, independent thinking, and just plain human orneriness*

Behaviorism: *A psychological movement, now extinct, that is built on the premise that you are what you do, and you do because of what you have done. Replaced by humanistic psychology (you are what you feel), cognitive science (you are what you think), Dr. Atkins (you are what you eat) and modern advertising (you are what we say).*

Ultimately, our lives and livelihoods are all in the hands of economists, and we are all economists or more specifically, sales people, because we must understand and learn how to master the transactions that make the world tick, and learn the art of persuasion. For economists, incentive is a simple thing. Economists assume that humans are utility maximizing creatures, and that the value or 'decision utility' of what you are doing in the moment corresponds with what you are expecting to do in the future. Drive to the store and the utility of each moment in the car matches that of the destination. The destination in other words 'pulls' you in its direction, and your motivation is in turn determined by the end point alone. This 'rational expectations' model makes economic forecasting easy. Just arrange incentives just so, and humans will carom back and forth the economic landscape in logical and predictable order. For the sales person, the implications of economics are clear.

Incentives are the cornerstone of modern life, and understanding incentives-or, often ferreting them out- is the key to solving just about any riddle, from violent crime to sports cheating to online dating. Behavior is always 'right' or in other words occurs because of incentives and disincentives both obvious and subtle. Identify and control them, and you are on the path to success, and do so better than the other person and you are on the path to great success.

The conventional wisdom is often wrong- Sales don't occur because of clever closing questions, interminable cold calls, or human kindness. They occur because of qualified introduction, explanation and challenge, and the delivery of value for value. Sales is not inherently stressful, or fearful, or frustrating, but is inadvertently arranged to be so.

Dramatic effects have distant, even subtle, causes- *"The answer to a riddle is not always right in front of you."* It could be as simple as a polite introduction, or a well-designed business network.

"Experts" use their informational advantage to serve their own agendas.

Look not to the expert's knowledge and credentials, but to his vested interest. He likely answers to his paycheck first, then you. Perverse incentives are much more common than you think.

The Bane of Incentive

These observations are unremarkable, but are troubling nonetheless because they reduce human agency to external events. That can be a scary thing. If incentives work, then human agency, and in particular free agency or freedom is in someone else's control. That's a dangerous notion because as it empowers people who want to influence others (you the salesperson), it dis-empowers those who don't want to be influenced. Incentive motivation means folks are pliable, and thus can be made to do anything.

This is the problem of the behaviorist movement that in the late 50's and 60's championed the importance of extrinsic rewards of reinforcers in the prediction and control of human behavior. It didn't address emotion in its equations, preferring instead to note the consistent correlations between behavior and rewards. This was of course micro-economics reduced from the transactional to the personal, with your behavior reduced to the mere equation of punishment and reward. But the problem for behaviorism, as it was for micro-economics, was that its predictions were not reliable. People did not behave the way they were supposed to, and did not pursue their logical interests as the economist and behaviorist expected they would. Because of this, the influence of behaviorism and micro-economics faded. They became relegated to second tier status behind those perspectives on human nature, from evolutionary psychology to self-determination theory (the intrinsic motivation folks) that restored human freedom to its dominant place in human nature. As we have seen from our review of the literature on business networking, this extends to our business natures as well.

The nascent rise of neurologically based theories of incentive motivation promises to change this perspective. By incorporating emotion or affect into the behaviorist's equation of motivation and the micro-economists concept of demand, it describes how sentiment derives from the social and business networks that we use. Starting logically, we all end up sentimental, as we begin to like and care about each other. The transaction is still of primary importance of course, but as all salespeople know, a sense of loyalty due to many transactions in the past can shade a client's judgment, and make them more likely to buy from you, or remain loyal to a current vendor who may serve them less well. This inverts the concept of 'givers gain' with the gain coming first, and the giving coming later.

As a better explanation for incentive motivation rises to the fore, it will change the face of networking, from the small networks we use to transact business, to the global networks upon which ride the future of the race. This change is already occurring, and will occur not only because of our intelligence, but also because of the intelligence of our tools.

The Future of Networking

"We'll know that computers are really smart when computers start getting bored. If you assign a computer a profoundly tedious task like spotting house numbers in video images, and then you come back a couple of hours later and find that the computer is checking its Facebook feed or surfing porn, then you'll know that artificial intelligence has fully arrived."- Nicolas Carr

What's the future of office productivity? Google giving you the tools.

What's the future of knowledge? Google informing you.

What's the future of transportation? Google driving you.

What's the present of the web? Google driving you nuts.

What's the future of the web? Google turning itself off.

When money is involved, even the most virtuous of us can go bad. It is difficult to argue against one's paycheck, and people therefore don't argue, preferring instead to rationalize rather than to reason. Google seems to be the exception, and its overweening purpose seems not to aggregate knowledge but to advise you on the knowledge you should consume. Its next logical step is to advise you *when* to consume it, and just maybe backing up its advice with action, with the proper permissions of course. Google's new service 'Google Now' promises to get you 'the right information at just the right time' through algorithmically examining your historical decisions using the search engine. This is but one-step away from proactively determining and *enforcing* what is best for you, like a caring concierge, even though it may be uncomfortable and disorienting, as the next example illustrates.

In an episode of the science fiction anthology 'The Outer Limits', a computerized avatar concierge noticed that all the automated features of the apartment complex were making people dependent and not interdependent, with people literally dying unattended in the halls, no doubt to be sucked up the next day by an auto-vac. Therefore, it remedied the situation, as all good concierges do for bad customers, by simply withholding service. Being forced to fend for themselves as well as escape from the now inoperative building and surrounding city (obviously computerized concierges are all of one over-mind about this), the episode ended with people stumbling out into the light of day, forced to deal with a new and refreshing uncertainty.

In this networked world, we are beginning to lose our sense of identity, self, and even place, and that is because we have lost our sense of timing of when and where to access information. Simply put, our motivational clocks are off. Not only do we not have a sense of timing, we don't know how to use timing to not only improve our own behavior but that of others. A case may be made that they have always been off. In the past, incentives were haphazard and poor. Today they are haphazard and good, too good, and we cannot time or consume them in the proper intervals because they are affective and addictive things. Like a car whose timing is off causes backfires, fits and starts, and makes us mad, networks without correct timing will proverbially backfire and have fits and starts, and ultimately drive us mad. It is as if we were traveling along on the highway, only to stop every five minutes to check the tires, windshield, oil, and direction. Life is not on cruise control but is comprised of an endless series of small lurches, and as we described earlier, this can be devastating to our productivity and our mental and physical health.

Perhaps Google can save us, but more likely, we must do the job ourselves, and when we do business networks will be only one part of the equation.

Virtuous Worlds

Business sales cultures are dependent upon successful networking, and so is every other social institution that makes our civilization thrive. The proper design of social and business networks mandates obsession, the positive affect that makes accomplishment supreme and that echoes in eternity. Freud got it right when he said happiness is the ability to love and do productive work, but he neglected to say that bliss is to raise such things to the level of obsession. Meaningful cultural design must aim to raise love to passion, and productivity to a sense of accomplishment that resonates not for a time but for all time. Humans are not evolved to be passive, our heaven is obsession that is guided and rewarded by meaning.

The future of networks and networking implicates the intelligent design of culture to spur motivation, but also to create meaning. A Monet is worth the money because it is resonant with 'meaning', the affective priming effect that occurs when we consider its branching and surprising implications. Life is transactional, and virtue only means you can't see the strings. But virtue emerges from social networks run well.

We start our selfish. We look out from our cribs and with wide eyes silently ask, what can you do for me? If we don't get our way, we will just scream. Then, in time, your mood changes. Your demand mentality becomes sentimentality, and that old couch, toy, friend, or parent, all useless, worn, and decrepit, become more valuable than gold. Who would have thought that the simplest spur for our sentiments and private virtue come from playing with a teddy bear, sitting on a couch, and visiting parents on Christmas?

We live not just to do useful things, but to maximize them. We want to be accomplished, rich, and wise, with loved ones and lovers aplenty. We also want to not just anticipate our pleasures but take them in the moment. Oftentimes, a momentary pleasure fortifies and secures a value in the future. Pleasure in one's labor as it uncertainly leads to a positive outcome means you can figuratively have your cake and eat it too. Maximizing future outcomes as you maximize the pleasure of present outcomes is permanent bliss, happiness even. To love and do productive work are things to be proud of, the pleasures that come from reminiscence of the past and a projection of the future. Virtue is wholly irrational, yet we are quite comfortable with that fact, as it comes from the explanations we use and the networks we weave.

Index

References

References: A psychological garnish or list of indigestible citations found at the end of books or scholarly articles that prove that the author did his homework and therefore must have his cloddish ideas be taken more seriously than your unreferenced common sense.

[1] Gladstones, W. H.; Regan, M. A.; Lee, R. B. (1989). "Division of attention: The single-channel hypothesis revisited". *Quarterly Journal of Experimental Psychology: Human Experimental Psychology* **41** (A): 1–17.

[2] Pashler, H. (1994). Dual task interference in simple tasks: Data and Theory. *Psychological Bulletin* **116** (2): 220–244

[3] Mayer, R. E., & Moreno, R. (2003). Nine ways to reduce cognitive load in multimedia learning. *Educational Psychologist*, 38(1), 43-52.

[4] Junco, R. & Cotten, S. (2010). Perceived academic effects of instant messaging use. *Computers & Education*, 56(2), 370-378.

[5] Basex.com

[6] Mark, G., Gonzalez, V., and Harris, J. No Task Left Behind? Examining the Nature of Fragmented Work. *Proceedings of CHI'05*, (2005), 113-120

[7] Boorstin, D. (1992) *The Creators*. New York: Random House

[8] Economist article on business pedagogy

[9] Wikipedia

[10] Pink. D. (2011) *Drive: The Surprising Truth About What Motivates Us.* Riverhead Trade

[11] Shirky, C. (2010) *Cognitive Surplus Cognitive Surplus: Creativity and Generosity in a Connected Age.* Penguin Press, New York

[12] Kaplan, F. , Oudeyer, P. (2007) In search of neural circuits of intrinsic motivation, *Frontiers in Neuroscience*, 1(1), 225-236

ABOUT THE AUTHOR

A. J. Marr lives alone in a large house in the middle of a hundred-acre wood with his two cats somewhere in Southeast Louisiana. As of this moment, he still does not know how to operate his VCR, which is obsolete anyways. He can be contacted at artm@benecominc.com

And if you like/dislike this book, then you are certain to like/dislike the other eight books I have written while languishing in my solitary confines. My web site Doctor Mezmer links to all my books and other assorted scribblings, which you can read entire with the only investment being your very precious time.

https://www.doctormezmer.com/books